S T A T E   P U B L

GLOUCESTER - CHELTF

ISHOPS CLEEVE · QUEDGELEY · SHURDING

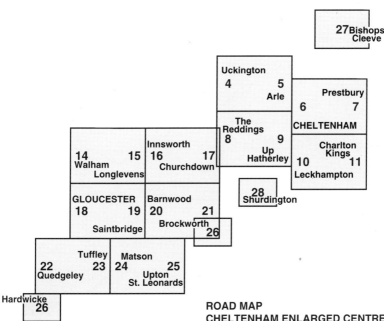

						27 Bishops Cleeve	
		Uckington 4	5 Arle	6	Prestbury 7		
		The Reddings 8	9	CHELTENHAM			
14 Walham	15	Innsworth 16	17	Up Hatherley	10	Charlton Kings 11	
Longlevens		Churchdown			Leckhampton		
GLOUCESTER 18	19	Barnwood 20	21	28 Shurdington			
Saintbridge		Brockworth 26					
Tuffley	23	Matson 24	25				
22 Quedgeley		Upton St. Leonards					
Hardwicke 26							

ROAD MAP — Page 2-3
CHELTENHAM ENLARGED CENTRE — Page 12
GLOUCESTER ENLARGED CENTRE — Page 13
INDEX TO STREETS — Page 28

Every effort has been made to verify the accuracy of information in this book but the publishers cannot accept responsibility for expense or loss caused by an error or omission. Information that will be of assistance to the user of the maps will be welcomed.

The representation on these maps of a road, track or path is no evidence of the existence of a right of way.

Car Park	P
Public Convenience	C
Place of Worship	+
One-way Street	→
Pedestrianized	▨
Post Office	●

Scale of street plans 4 inches to 1 mile
Unless otherwise stated

Street plans prepared and published by ESTATE PUBLICATIONS, Bridewell House, TENTERDEN, KENT, and based upon the ORDNANCE SURVEY mapping with the permission of The Controller of H. M. Stationery Office.

The Publishers acknowledge the co-operation of the local authorities of towns represented in this atlas.

state Publications 242 H   ISBN 1 84192 061 4   © Crown Copyright 398713

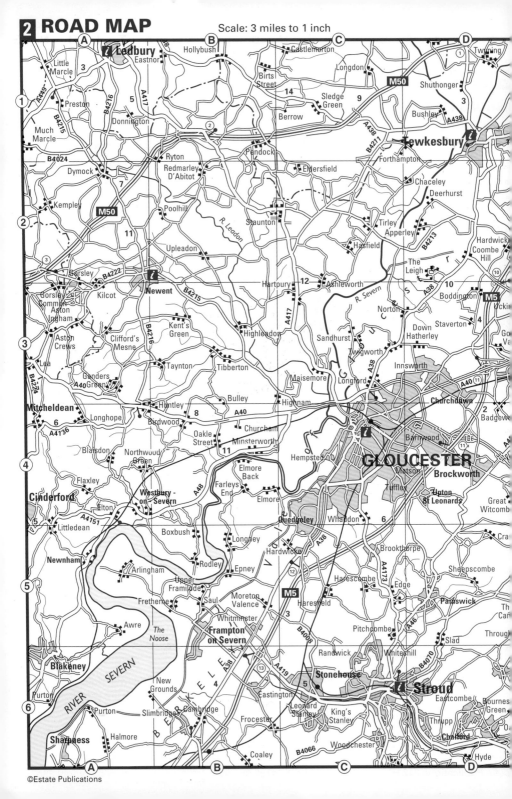

2 ROAD MAP

Scale: 3 miles to 1 inch

©Estate Publications

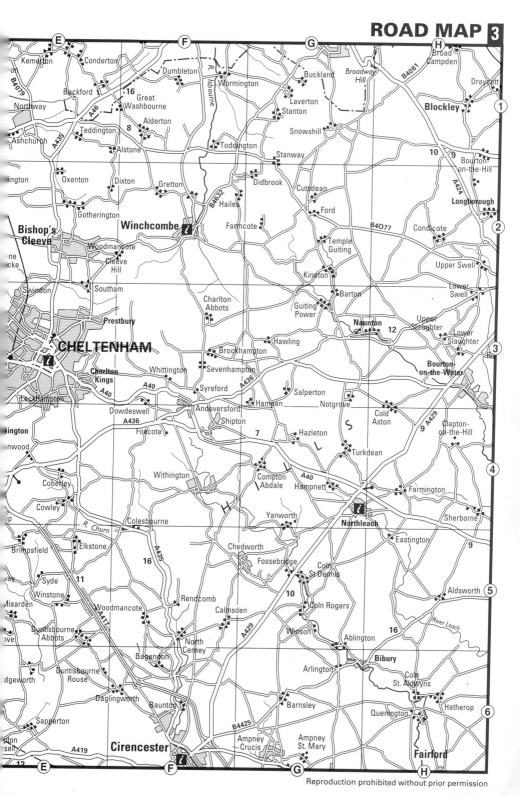

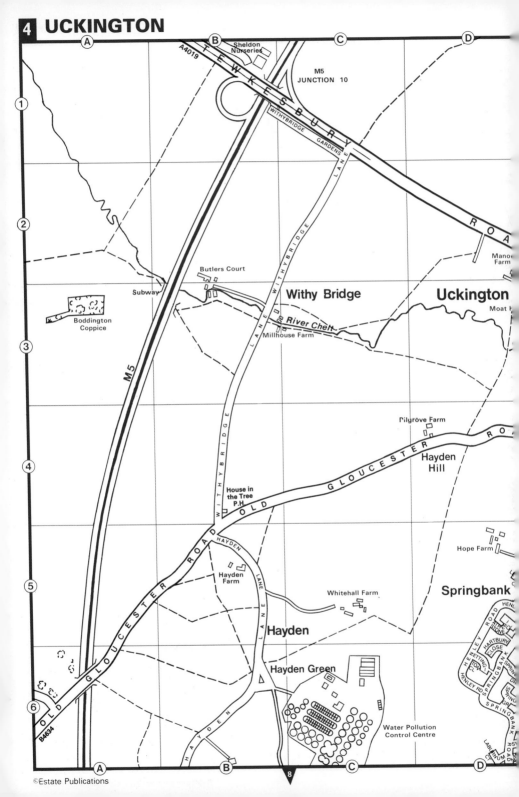

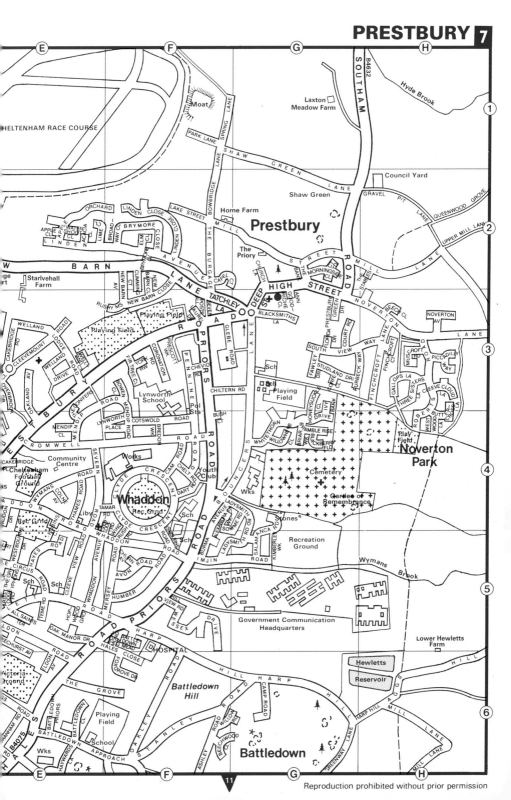

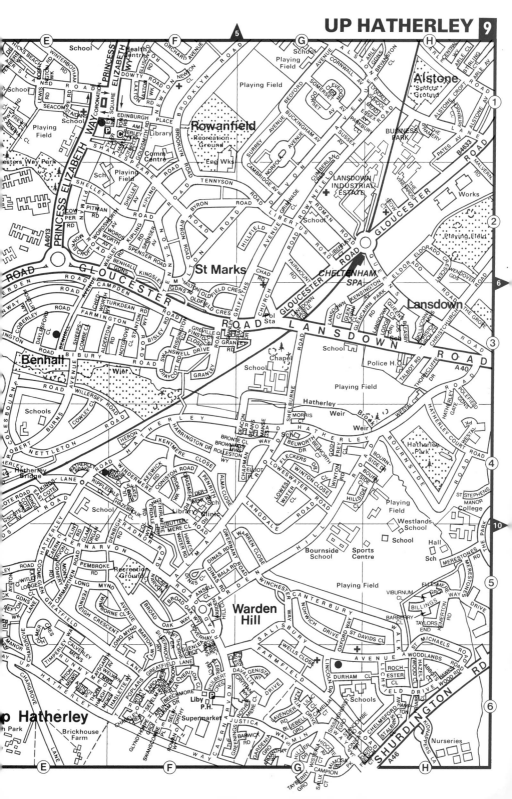

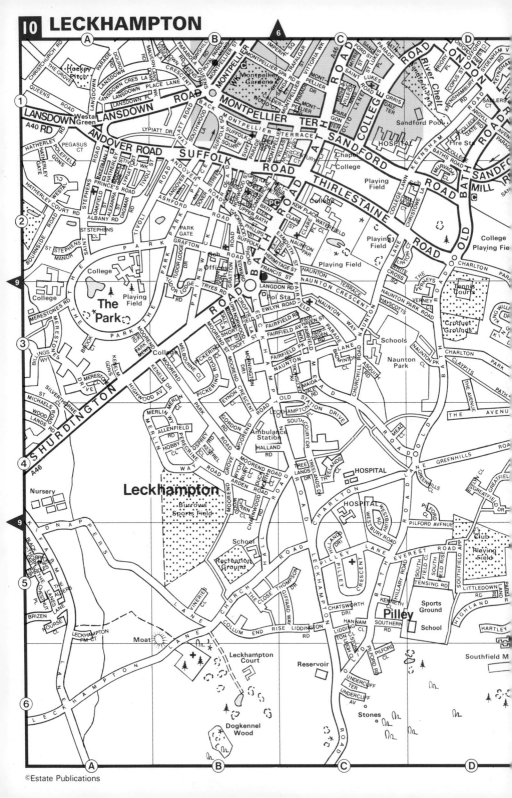

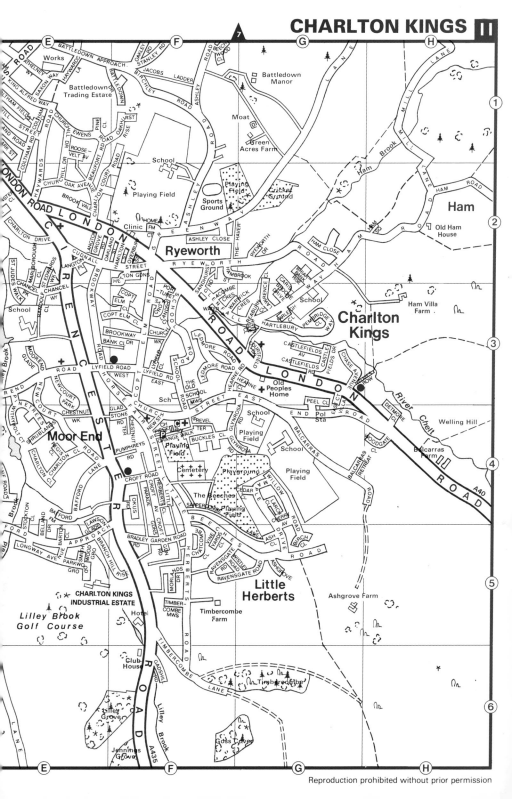

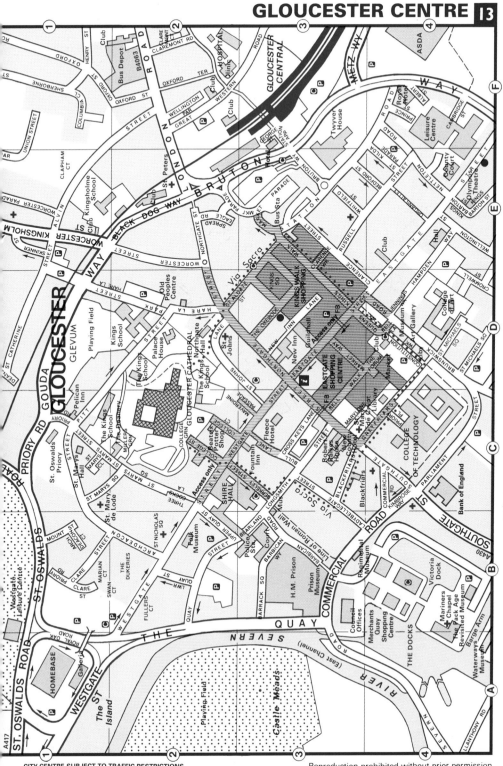

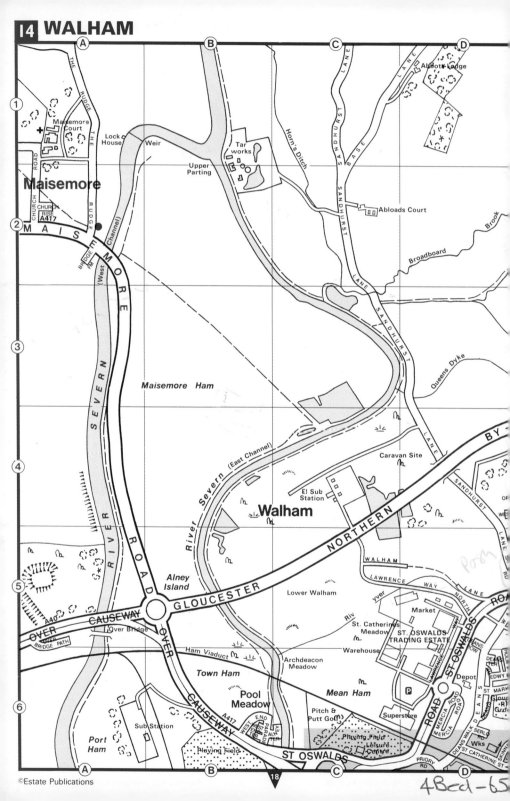

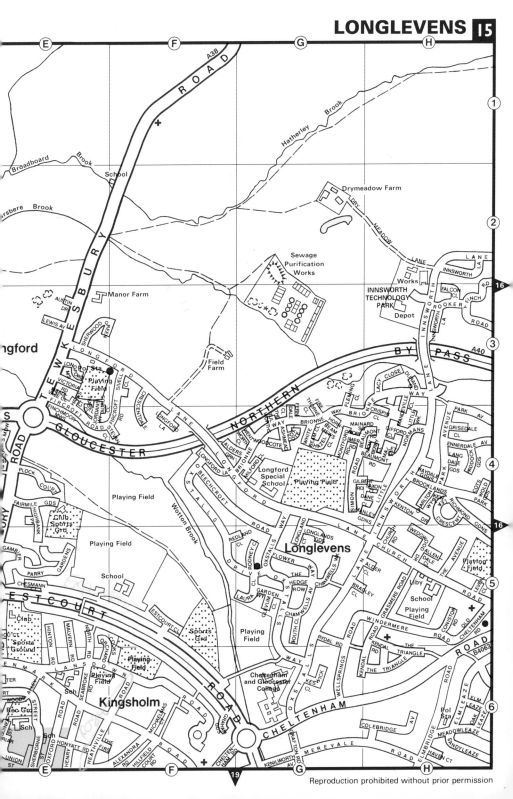

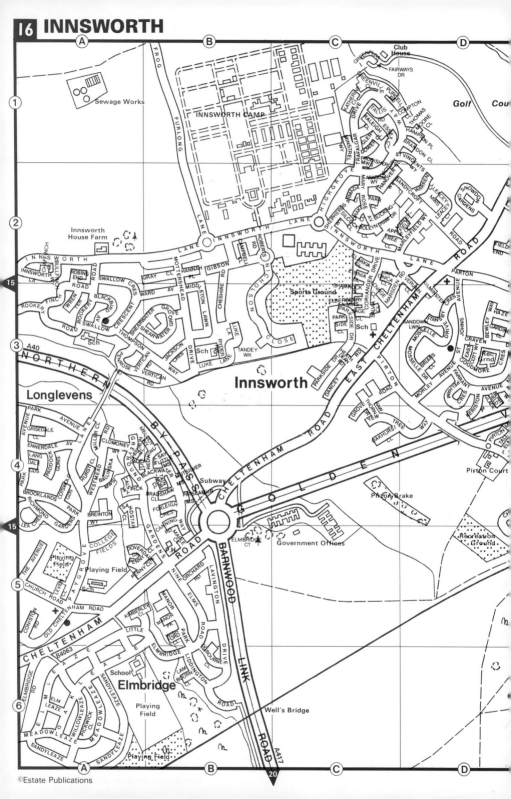

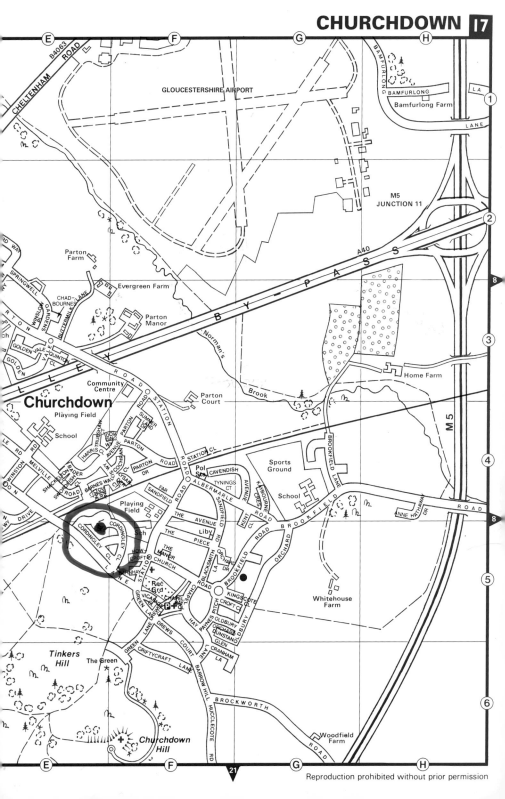

GLOUCESTERSHIRE AIRPORT

BAMFURLONG

Bamfurlong Farm

LA

LANE

M5
JUNCTION 11

B4063 ROAD
CHELTENHAM ROAD

SPRINGWELL GARDENS

Parton Farm

Evergreen Farm

CHAD-
BOURNES
BUTTERMILK LANE

Parton Manor

Norman's

Brook

Home Farm

GOLDEN VALE
GOLDEN

Community Centre

Parton Court

M 5

Churchdown

Playing Field

School

STATION ROAD

SUMMER

Sports Ground

School

BROOKFIELD LANE

ROAD

ANNE HATHAWAY DR

HARRIS CL
TRUBSHAW
AVENUE
PARTON
PARTON DR

Pol Sta

CAVENDISH
TYNINGS CT

BARNES WAY
COCHRAN
SANDY
FAR SANDFIELD

ALBERMARLE
SANDFIELD

AVENUE

KENT RD
KYBOURNE CREST

BROOKFIELD
ORCHARD

Playing Field

THE AVENUE
THE PIECE

Liby

THE MANOR

ORCHARD DR

BLACKSMITH LA
Whitehouse Farm

HOW

CROFT
CHURCH

VICARAGE

Rec Grd

STATION GREEN

CHAPEL

KINGSCOTE
CROFT CL

OLDBURY
DUNSTANO
DUNSBURY

PITCH
HAY

DREWS
CRIFTYCRAFT LANE

GREEN LANE
BARROW HILL

CHAPEL
ROAD

PAYNE
ORCHARD
GLEN

CRANHAM LA

Tinkers Hill

The Green

BROCKWORTH

HUCCLECOTE
RD

Woodfield Farm

ROAD

Churchdown Hill

21

Reproduction prohibited without prior permission

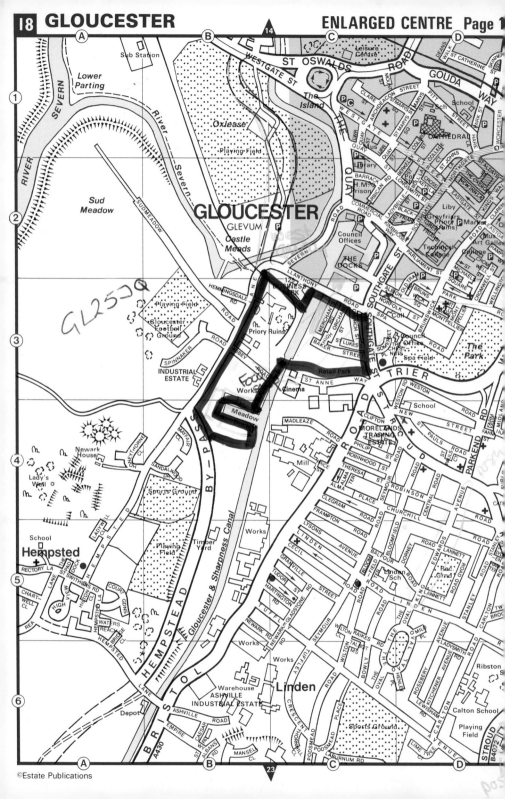

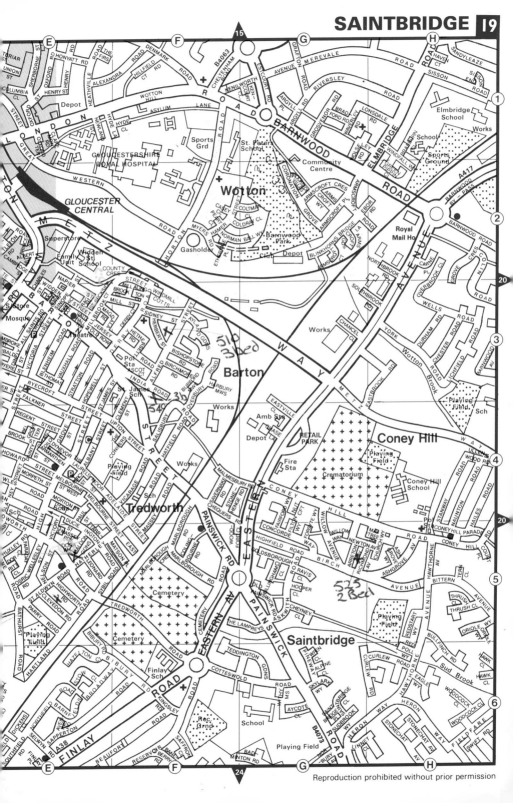

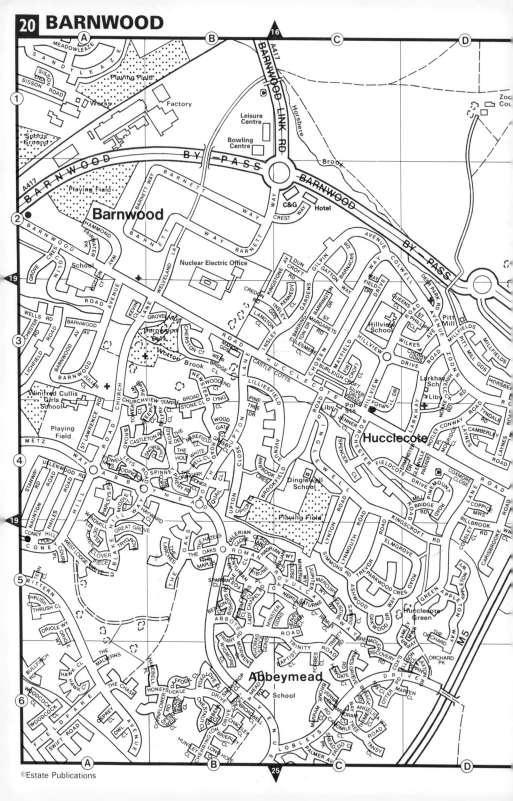

20 BARNWOOD

Barnwood

Hucclecote

Abbeymead

©Estate Publications

Reservoir

SOLDIERS WALK

Reservoir

The Brake

Churchdown Hill

The Coombs

Covered Reservoir

HUCCLECOTE LANE

LANE

M5

BROCKWORTH ROAD

Woodlands Farm

Pressmead Farm

Noake Court Farm

CHURCHDOWN

Junction 11A

Dean Farm

Roman Villa (site of)

A417

CEDAR ROAD

MAPLE ROAD

GARDENS

Horsbere Brook

Brockwarth Court

BROCKWORTH ROAD

Brockworth

Playing Field

SUSSEX GARDENS

COLERNE DRIVE

SUSSEX GARDENS

HUCCLECOTE

HUCCLECOTE ROAD

MONTGOMERY CL

GRIEFLON CL

JAMES CT

FOLLAND AV

FOLLAND AV

BY PASS

ERMIN

ROWAN

WESTFIELD ROAD

WESTFIELD

PRINCE ALBERT CT

ASTOR CL

Post Stn

GOLF CLUB LA

ERMIN

HILLVIEW AV

PARK ELM DR

OAK DRIVE

BOVERTON DRIVE

BOVERTON

BOVERTON DRIVE

PARK AVENUE

ST ANNES CL

ANSON DR

FAIRHAVEN CT

DRIVE

RIDGEMOUNT CL

VICARAGE CT

SAYERS CRES

HICKLEY GDNS

TANNERS

HURCOMBE WAY CL

Liby

MILL LANE

TAMAR RD

CLYDE

TRENT ROAD

LEADON CL

SEVERN RD

MEDWAY

WENT CL

LEA ROAD

Mill Farm

LANE

Sports Ground

Sch

TAMAR ROAD

WAY CR

GLOUCESTER TRADING ESTATE

Works

STREET GREEN

GREEN ST

SEABROOK RD

GREEN BK

WAY

ABBOTSWOOD

SHERRET

MOORFIELD

GATER

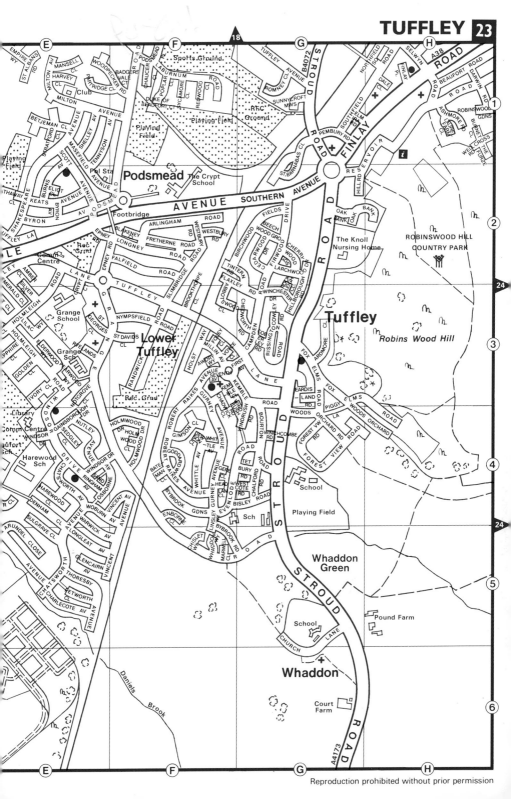

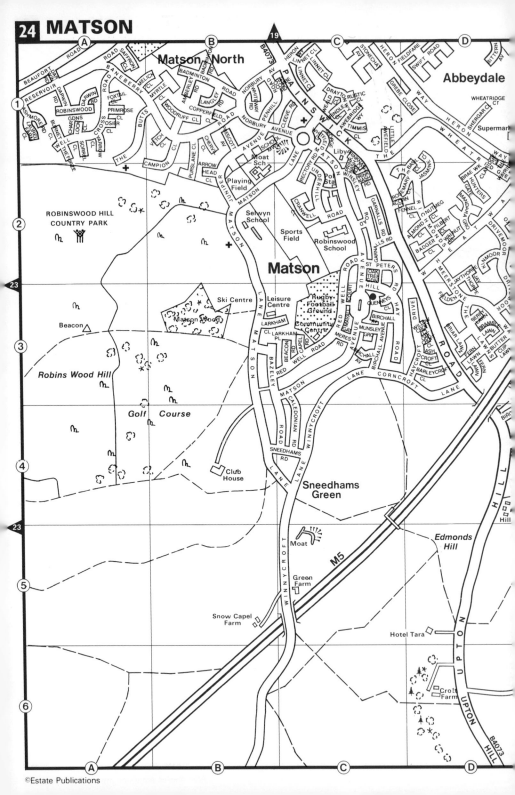

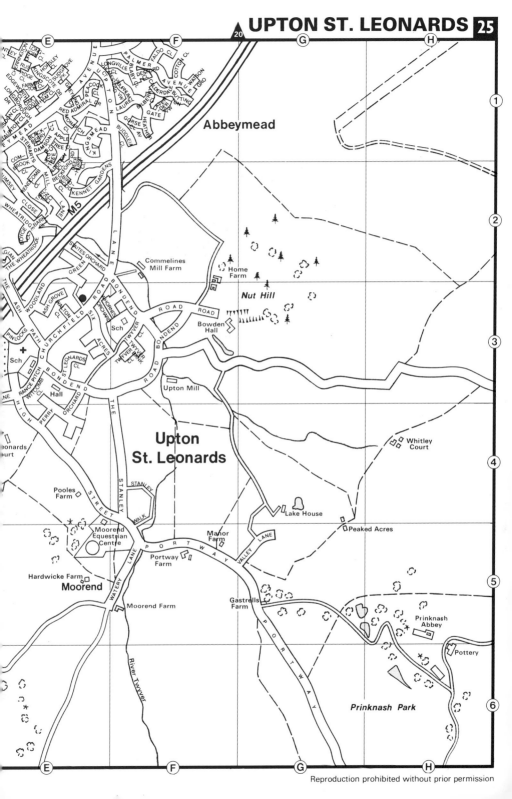

Abbeymead

Commelines
Mill Farm

Home
Farm

Nut Hill

Bowden
Hall

Upton Mill

Upton
St. Leonards

Whitley
Court

Pooles
Farm

Lake House

Peaked Acres

Moorend
Equestrian
Centre

Manor
Farm

Portway
Farm

Hardwicke Farm
Moorend

Moorend Farm

Gastrells
Farm

Prinknash
Abbey

Pottery

River Twyver

Prinknash Park

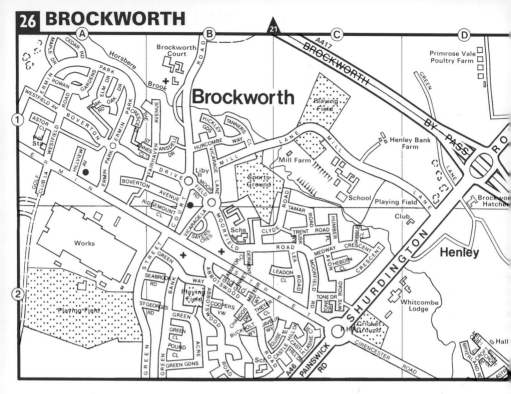

Brockworth

HARDWICKE

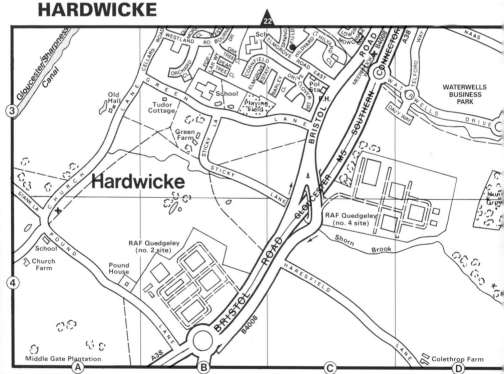

Hardwicke

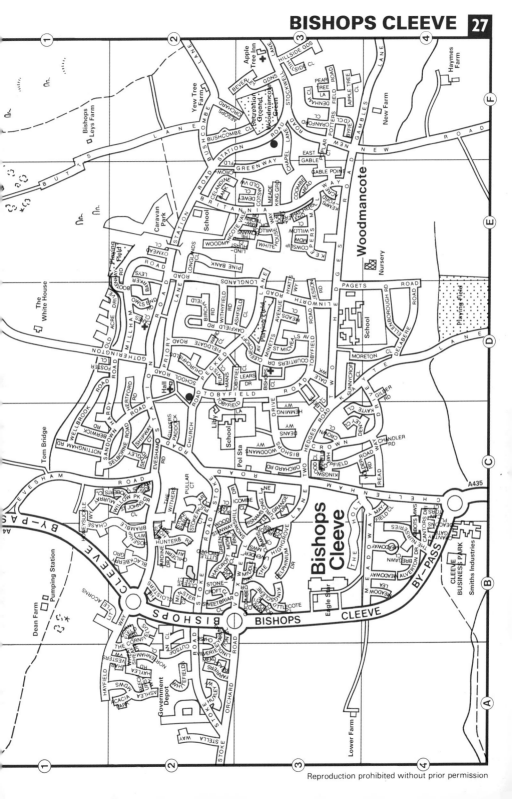

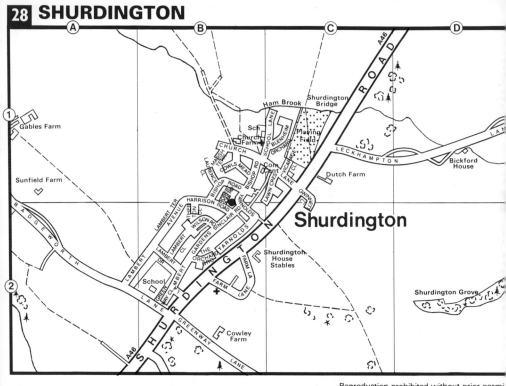

Shurdington

A - Z INDEX TO STREETS
with Postcodes

The Index includes some names for which there is insufficient space on the maps. These names are preceded by an * and are followed by the nearest adjoining thoroughfare.

BISHOPS CLEEVE

Abbots Mws. GL52	27 B4
Acacia Pk. GL52	27 A2
Aesops Orchard. GL52	27 F2
Alverton Dri. GL52	27 B4
Anderson Clo. GL52	27 E3
Apple Tree Clo. GL52	27 F3
Ashfield Clo. GL52	27 D3
Ashlea Meadows. GL52	27 A2
Barker Leys. GL52	27 D2
Beechurst Way. GL52	27 F3
Berwick Rd. GL52	27 C1
Beverley Gdns. DL52	27 F3
Birchfield Rd. GL52	27 D2
Bishops Cleeve	
By-Pass. GL52	27 B2
Bishops Clo. GL52	27 C3
Bishops Dri. GL52	27 C3
Bishops Mdw. GL52	27 B2
Blackberry Gro. GL52	27 B2
Bootenhay Rd. GL52	27 D2
Bramble Chase. GL52	27 B2
Bregawn Clo. GL52	27 B4
Britannia Way. GL52	27 F2
Buckland Clo. GL52	27 C2
Bushcombe Clo. GL52	27 F2
Bushcombe La. GL52	27 F2
Butts La. GL52	27 E1

Byfield Clo. GL52	27 F3
Cantors Ct. GL52	27 C4
Cantors Dri. GL52	27 B4
Cares Clo. GL52	27 D2
Celandine Bank. GL52	27 E2
Chandler Rd. GL52	27 C4
Chantry Gate. GL52	27 B4
Chapel La. GL52	27 E3
Charlcote Corner. GL52	27 B3
Cheltenham Rd. GL52	27 C4
Chiltern Av. GL52	27 B2
Church Rd. GL52	27 C2
Churchfields. GL52	27 D2
Cleeve Ct. GL52	27 C3
Cleeve Lake Ct. GL52	27 C4
Cleevecroft Av. GL52	27 D3
Clematis Ct. GL52	27 B3
Coombe Meade. GL52	27 E3
Cornfield Dri. GL52	27 B2
Cotswold Vw. GL52	27 E3
Courtiers Dri. GL52	27 D3
Cowslip Meadow. GL52	27 E3
Cranford Clo. GL52	27 F3
Crowfield. GL52	27 E2
Crown Clo. GL52	27 C3
Crown Dri. GL52	27 C3
Cutsdean Clo. GL52	27 A2
Dale Walk. GL52	27 D3
Deacons Pl. GL52	27 C4
Deans Way. GL52	27 C3
Delabere Rd. GL52	27 D4
Delphinium Dri. GL52	27 B3
Denham Clo. GL52	27 F3
Denley Clo. GL52	27 C3
Dewey Clo. GL52	27 E3
East Gable. GL52	27 F3
Ellenborough Rd. GL52	27 D4
Evesham Rd. GL52	27 C1

Farriers Reach. GL52	27 A2
Fieldgate Rd. GL52	27 D2
Foster Clo. GL52	27 D1
Fox Moor. GL52	27 B2
Furlong La. GL52	27 C3
Gable Point. GL52	27 E3
Gambles La. GL52	27 F3
Gatcombe Clo. GL52	27 B3
Gilder Rd. GL52	27 D4
Gilders Paddock. GL52	27 C2
Gotherington La. GL52	27 D2
Grange Dri. GL52	27 C3
Green Meadow Bank.	
GL52	27 B2
Greenway. GL52	27 B2
Hardy Rd. GL52	27 C2
Harpfield Clo. GL52	27 C3
Harpfield Rd. GL52	27 C3
Harvesters View. GL52	27 A2
Hawthorn Dri. GL52	27 E3
Haycroft Clo. GL52	27 B2
Hayfield Way. GL52	27 B2
Haylea Rd. GL52	27 A2
Hemming Way. GL52	27 C3
Hertford Rd. GL52	27 D2
Hillside Clo. GL52	27 F3
Hillside Gdns. GL52	27 F3
Hisnams Field. GL52	27 C3
Holder Rd. GL52	27 C4
Honeysuckle Way.	
GL52	27 B1
Hunters Rd. GL52	27 B2
Huntsmans Clo. GL52	27 D2
Huxley Way. GL52	27 A2
Hyatts Way. GL52	27 D3
Icombe Clo. GL52	27 C3
INDUSTRIAL & RETAIL:	
Cleeve Business Pk.	

GL52	27 B4
Jardine Dri. GL52	27 B2
Jesson Rd. GL52	27 D3
Kayte Clo. GL52	27 C4
Kayte La. GL52	27 D3
Keepers Mill. GL52	27 E3
Kempsford Acre. GL52	27 B3
Kingsclere Dri. GL52	27 B3
Kingswood Clo. GL52	27 C3
Lavender Ms. GL52	27 C3
Lears Dri. GL52	27 D3
Lindhurst Clo. GL52	27 E3
Lindley Chase. GL52	27 A2
Linworth Rd. GL52	27 D3
Little Acorns. GL52	27 B1
Little Orchard. GL52	27 B2
Littlecote Clo. GL52	27 B3
Longlands Clo. GL52	27 E2
Longlands Rd. GL52	27 D3
Marlborough Clo. GL52	27 B3
Mayfield Clo. GL52	27 C4
Meade King Gro. GL52	27 E3
Meadow Lea. GL52	27 B4
Meadoway. GL52	27 B4
Meads Clo. GL52	27 D3
Middle Hay Ct. GL52	27 B3
Millham Rd. GL52	27 D2
Minetts Av. GL52	27 D3
Minster Clo. GL52	27 B2
Moreton Clo. GL52	27 D4
Murray Clo. GL52	27 C2
New Rd. GL52	27 F3
Nortenham Clo. GL52	27 A2
Nottingham Rd. GL52	27 C1
Oakfield Rd. GL52	27 D2
Old Acre Dri. GL52	27 D2
Orchard Rd. GL52	27 C3
Owls End Rd. GL52	27 D2

Oxmead Clo. GL52	
Pagets Rd. GL52	
Pear Tree La. GL52	
Pecked La. GL52	
Pine Bank. GL52	
Poplar Dri. GL52	
Potters Field Rd. GL52	
Priory La. GL52	
Pullar Clo. GL52	
Pullar Ct. GL52	
Read Way. GL52	
Roberts Clo. GL52	
Rosehip Way. GL52	
St Johns Clo. GL52	
St Michaels Av. GL52	
School Rd. GL52	
Sedgley Rd. GL52	
Selbourne Rd. GL52	
Shipway Ct. GL52	
Snowshill Dri. GL52	
Station Rd. GL52	
Stella Way. GL52	
Stockwell La. GL52	
Stoke Orchard Rd. GL52	
Stoke Park Clo. GL52	
Stoke Park Ct. GL52	
Stoke Rd. GL52	
Stonecroft Clo. GL52	
Streamside. GL52	
Sunnycroft Clo. GL52	
Sweetbriar Clo. GL52	
Thatchers End. GL52	
The Cloisters. GL52	
The Cornfield. GL52	
The Highgrove. GL52	
The Holt. GL52	
The Nurseries. GL52	

wans. GL52 27 E3
thers. GL52 27 C2
ild Clo. GL52 27 D3
ild La. GL52 27 D2
ild Rd. GL52 27 D2
edges Rd. GL52 27 C3
e Mead. GL52 27 A2
l La. GL52 27 B3
Clo. GL52 27 D2
ook Rd. GL52 27 C1
sheaf Dri. GL52 27 A2
ouse Way. GL52 27 E3
elds. GL52 27 A2
r Dri. GL52 27 E3
Clo. GL52 27 E3
Park Dri. GL52 27 C2
eld Rd. GL52 27 D2
nancote Vale.
          27 E2
hans Way. GL52 27 C3
anway Dri. GL52 27 B2
ton Clo. GL52 27 B2

HELTENHAM

Clo. GL51 9 H6
Clo. GL52 7 E2
Ct. GL51 8 D1
Cres. GL52 11 F3
Rd. GL51 6 A3
l Clo. GL51 9 E1
ill. GL54 7 H6
Rd. GL50 10 A2
arle Gate. GL50 6 C3
Dri. GL52 6 D2
Pl. GL52 6 D5
Rd. GL52 6 D4
St. GL50 6 C4
Pl. GL52 12 D2
St. GL52 12 C2
Walk. GL50 12 C2
naw Clo. GL51 9 E5
n Rd. GL51 9 E3
e Clo. GL50 6 B4
dra St. GL50 6 A3
dra La Walk. GL52 7 F4
ats Rd. GL52 6 D5
ats Ter. GL52 7 E5
ats Villas Rd. GL52 6 D5
eld Rd. GL53 10 B4
lo. GL51 9 F4
d. GL51 9 F5
d Ct. GL51 8 D1
Rd. GL51 9 H1
Croft. GL51 9 H1
r La. GL51 5 G6
ey Rd. GL51 9 F1
se Pl. GL50 12 B2
se St. GL50 12 A2
Clo. GL50 6 A5
r Rd. GL50 10 A1
r St. GL50 10 B2
r Walk. GL50 10 B2
Ct. GL52 6 D4
oodriche Clo.
          7 G3
Clo. GL51 9 F5
Clo. GL52 7 E2
Orchard. GL52 7 E2
n Av. GL51 8 C5
Rd. GL53 10 B4
Rd. GL53 10 D1
edge Rd. GL52 7 E5
lo. GL50 6 B2
GL51 6 A4
. GL51 6 A4
Rd. GL53 8 D3
. GL51 5 G6
Ins. GL51 5 H6
. GL51 5 G5
am. GL51 9 F6
ha. GL51 9 G6
. GL53 11 G5
Mews. GL51 9 E6
d Rd. GL50 10 B2
ve. GL53 11 G5
ds Clo. GL51 5 E5
ds Rd. GL51 5 E5
Clo. GL52 11 F2
Rd. GL52 7 F6
Rd. GL53 10 C3
Gro. GL51 8 D1
y Way. GL52 11 E1
one Clo. GL51 4 D5
Clo. GL51 5 F4

Avenell Par. GL53 10 D1
Avon Rd. GL52 7 F5
Aylton Clo. GL51 9 E5
Aysgarth Av. GL51 9 E6
Azalea Dri. GL51 9 G6

Back Albert Pl. GL52 6 D5
Back Montpellier Ter. GL50 12 A6
Badgeworth Rd. GL51 8 B5
Badminton Clo. GL53 10 C3
Bafford App. GL53 11 E5
Bafford Farm. GL53 11 E4
Bafford Gro. GL53 11 E5
Bafford La. GL53 11 E4
Bakehouse La. GL50 10 A2
Baker St. GL51 6 B4
Bala Rd. GL51 9 F5
Balcarras Retreat. GL53 11 G4
Balcarras Rd. GL53 11 G4
Ballinode Clo. GL50 6 A2
Bamfurlong La. GL51 8 A3
Bank Clo. GL53 11 E3
Bank Clo. GL51 5 E5
Barberry Clo. GL50 9 H5
Barbridge Rd. GL51 5 F6
Barley Clo. GL51 5 E4
Barlow Rd. GL51 5 F5
Barnards Row. GL50 12 A2
Barnett Clo. GL51 5 E4
Barratts Mill La. GL53 12 D4
Barrington Av. GL51 8 C 4
Barton Clo. GL53 11 E5
Barton Way. GL51 9 F5
Barwick Rd. GL51 9 G6
Bath Par. GL53 12 C6
Bath Rd. GL53 12 C6
Bath St. GL50 12 C4
Bath Ter. GL50 10 B2
Bathville Mws. GL53 12 C6
Battledown App. GL52 7 E6
Battledown Clo. GL52 7 E6
Battledown Dri. GL52 11 E1
Battledown Mead. GL52 7 F5
Battledown Priors. GL52 7 E6
Baynham Way. GL50 12 B2
Bayshill La. GL50 12 A4
Bayshill Rd. GL50 12 A5
Beale Rd. GL51 5 E6
Beale Walk. GL51 5 E6
Beaufort Rd. GL52 11 E2
Beaumont Dri. GL51 5 E5
Beaumont Rd. GL51 5 E5
Bedford Av. GL51 9 G1
Beech Clo. GL52 7 H3
Beeches Rd. GL53 11 F4
Beechmore Dri. GL51 9 F6
Beechurst Av. GL52 7 E5
Beechwood Clo. GL52 7 F6
Belland Dri. GK53 11 E5
Belmont Rd. GL52 6 D5
Belmore Pl. GL53 12 C5
Belworth Ct. GL51 9 G4
Belworth Dri. GL51 9 G4
Benhall Av. GL52 9 E3
Benhall Gdns. GL51 9 F2
Bennington St. GL50 12 C2
Berkeley Pl. GL52 6 D6
Berkeley St. GL52 6 D6
Bethesda. GL50 10 B2
Beverley Croft. GL51 8 D1
Bibury Rd. GL51 9 E3
Billings Way. GL50 9 H5
Birch Clo. GL53 11 G5
Birchley Rd. GL52 11 F1
Bishopstone Clo. GL51 8 D2
Bisley Rd. GL51 9 F3
Blackberry Field. GL52 7 G4
Blacksmiths La. GL52 7 G3
Blackthorn End. GL53 10 A5
Bladon Mews. GL51 8 C4
Blaisdon Way. GL51 5 E4
Blake Croft. GL51 5 E4
Bleasby Gdns. GL51 9 H3
Blenheim Sq. GL51 5 F6
Bloomsbury St. GL50 6 B4
Bluebell Gro. GL51 9 G6
Bodnam Rd. GL51 5 F4
Boulton Rd. GL50 6 B2
Bouncers La. GL52 7 F4
Bournside Clo. GL51 9 H4
Bournside Dri. GL51 9 H4
Bournside Rd. GL51 9 H4
Bowbridge La. GL52 7 F2
Bowen Rd. GL52 7 F3
Bradley Rd. GL53 11 F5
Bramble Rise. GL52 7 G4

Bramley Rd. GL51 5 F5
Branch Hill Rise. GL53 11 E5
Branch Rd. GL51 8 B4
Brandon Pl. GL50 10 B2
Bredon Walk. GL52 7 F4
Brevel Ter. GL53 11 F4
Briar Rd. GL52 7 G4
Briarbank Rise. GL52 11 G2
Bridge St. GL51 6 A3
Bridgend Rd. GL51 8 D4
Brighton Rd. GL52 6 D6
Brizen La. GL53 10 A5
Broad Oak Way. GL51 9 F5
Broadway Clo. GL52 7 F2
Bronte Clo. GL51 9 F4
Brook Ct. GL50 10 A3
Brook Rd. GL51 5 H5
Brook Vale. GL52 11 E2
Brookfield Rd. GL3 8 A6
Brooklyn Clo. GL51 5 G5
Brooklyn Gdns. GL51 5 G5
Brooklyn Rd. GL51 9 F1
Brooksdale La. GL53 10 B3
Brookway Dri. GL53 11 F3
Brookway Rd. GL53 11 E2
Brown Clo. GL51 5 E5
Brownings Mews. GL51 9 F4
Brunswick St. GL50 6 C4
Bryaston Clo. GL51 5 H6
Brymore Av. GL52 7 F2
Brymore Clo. GL52 7 F2
Bryony Bank. GL53 10 A5
Buckingham Av. GL51 9 G1
Buckles Clo. GL53 11 F4
Bullingham Ct. GL51 6 B3
Burma Av. GL52 7 F5
Burton St. GL50 6 B5
Bush Ct. GL52 7 F4
Bushy Way. GL51 5 E4
Buttercross La. GL52 7 H4
Buttermere Clo. GL51 9 F5
Butts Walk. GL51 8 D4
Byron Rd. GL51 9 F2

Caernarvon Clo. GL51 9 F5
Caernarvon Ct. GL51 9 E5
Caernarvon Rd. GL51 9 E5
Cakebridge Pl. GL52 7 E4
Cakebridge Rd. GL52 7 E3
Calderwood Ct. GL50 12 B6
Calverley Mews. GL51 9 F4
Cam Rd. GL52 7 F4
Camberwell Rd. GL51 9 E1
Cambray Ct. GL50 12 C4
Cambray Pl. GL50 12 C4
Cambridge Av. GL51 9 G2
Camellia Ct. GL51 9 G6
Camp Rd. GL52 7 G6
Campden Rd. GL51 9 E3
Campion Park. GL51 9 G6
Canterbury Walk. GL51 9 G5
Capel Ct. GL52 7 F2
Carisbrook Dri. GL52 11 G3
Carlton Pl. GL51 6 B4
Carlton St. GL52 6 D6
Carlyle Rd. GL51 5 E4
Carmarthen Rd. GL51 9 E5
Carrol Gro. GL51 5 E5
Carter Rd. GL51 5 G4
Casino Pl. GL50 10 B2
Castlefields Av. GL52 11 G3
Castlefields Dri. GL52 11 G3
Castlefields Rd. GL52 11 G3
Castlemaine Dri. GL51 8 D3
Cedar Clo. GL53 11 G4
Cedar Court Rd. GL53 12 C6
Central Cross Dri. GL52 6 D4
Central Way. GL51 5 H6
Century Ct. GL51 10 C1
Chad Rd. GL51 9 G2
Chalford Av. GL51 8 C4
Chancel Pk. GL53 11 E3
Chancel Way. GL53 11 E3
Chapel La. GL50 10 B2
Chapel St. GL50 12 A2
Chapel Walk. GL50 12 B4
Chapman Way. GL51 9 G4
Chargrove La. GL51 9 E5
Charles St. GL50 6 B4
Charlton Clo. GL53 11 E2
Charlton Dri. GL53 11 E2
Charlton La. GL53 10 C4
Charlton Park Dri. GL53 10 D2
Charlton Park Gate. GL53 10 D3
Charnwood Clo. GL50 10 B4

Charnwood Rd. GL53 10 B4
Chase Av. GL52 11 G3
Chaseley Cres. GL51 9 F6
Chatcombe Clo. GL53 11 F5
Chatsworth Dri. GL53 10 C5
Chedworth Way. GL51 9 E3
Chelmsford Av. GL51 9 H6
Chelsea Clo. GL53 11 E2
Chelt Rd. GL52 7 F4
Chelt Walk. GL51 5 G5
Cheriton Clo. GL51 9 F6
Cherry Av. GL53 11 G4
Chester Walk. GL50 12 B2
Chestnut Pl. GL53 10 A5
Chestnut Ter. GL53 11 F4
Cheviot Rd. GL52 7 F3
Chestnut Walk. GL53 11 E4
Chiltern Rd. GL53 7 F3
Chosen View Rd. GL51 6 A2
Christchurch Ct. GL50 9 H3
Christchurch Rd. GL50 9 H3
Christowe La. GL53 10 D2
Church La. GL52 7 G2
Church Piece. GL53 11 F4
Church Rd,
Leckhampton. GL53 10 B5
Church Rd,
St Marks. GL51 9 G3
Church Rd,
Swindon. GL51 5 H2
Church St,
Charlton Kings. GL53 11 F4
Church St,
Cheltenham. GL50 12 B2
Church Walk. GL53 11 F3
Churchill Dri. GL52 11 E2
Churchill Rd. GL53 10 C3
Churn Av. GL52 7 F5
Cirencester Rd. GL53 11 E2
Clare Pl. GL53 10 C2
Clare St. GL53 10 C2
Clarence Par. GL50 12 B3
Clarence Rd. GL52 12 D1
Clarence Sq. GL50 12 C1
Clarence St. GL50 12 B2
Clarington Mws. GL50 6 C4
Clarke Way. GL50 6 B4
Claypits Path. GL53 10 D3
Cleeve Cloud La. GL52 7 H3
Cleeve View Rd. GL52 7 E5
Cleeveland St. GL51 6 B4
Cleevelands Av. GL50 6 C2
Cleevelands Clo. GL50 6 C2
Cleevelands Dri. GL50 6 C2
Cleevemont. GL50 6 C2
Cleevemount Clo. GL52 7 E3
Cleevemount Rd. GL52 7 E3
Clevedon Sq. GL51 9 G1
Clyde Cres. GL52 7 F4
Coberley Rd. GL51 9 E3
Cobham Rd. GL51 6 A4
Cobhams Ct. GL51 6 A4
Cold Pool La. GL51 8 C6
Colesbourne Rd. GL51 9 E4
College Baths Rd. GL53 10 D1
College Gate. GL53 10 D1
College Lawn. GL53 10 C2
College Rd. GL53 10 C1
Colletts Dri. GL51 6 A4
Collum End Rise. GL53 10 B5
Colne Av. GL51 7 E4
Coltham Clo. GL52 11 E1
Coltham Fields. GL52 11 E1
Coltham Rd. GL52 11 E1
Columbia St. GL52 6 D5
Colwyn Dri. GL51 9 F5
Commercial St. GL50 10 B2
Compton Rd. GL51 6 A3
Coniston Rd. GL51 9 F4
Coombe Glen La. GL51 9 E5
Coppice Gate. GL51 5 F3
Copt Elm Clo. GL53 11 F3
Copt Elm Rd. GL53 11 F3
Copus St. GL53 10 D1
Corfe Clo. GL51 7 G3
Cornmeadow Dri. GL51 5 E4
Cornwall Av. GL51 9 G1
Coronation Rd. GL52 7 F3
Coronation Sq. GL51 9 E1
Cotswold Rd. GL52 7 F4
Cottage Rake Av. GL50 6 B2
County Court Rd. GL52 12 C3
Court Rd. GL52 7 G3
Courtenay St. GL50 6 C4
Courtfield Dri. GL52 11 G3
Cowley Clo. GL51 9 E4
Cowper Rd. GL51 9 E2

Crabtree Pl. GL50 6 B4
Cranham Rd. GL52 7 E6
Crescent Pl. GL50 12 B3
Crescent Ter. GL50 12 B3
Croft Avenue Par. GL53 11 F4
Croft Gdns. GL53 11 F4
Croft La. GL53 10 B3
Croft Par. GL53 11 F4
Croft Rd. GL53 11 F4
Croft St. GL53 10 B3
Croft Thorne Clo. GL51 9 F5
Cromwell Rd. GL52 7 E4
Crythan Walk. GL51 9 G6
Cudnall St. GL53 11 E2
Culross Clo. GL50 6 D3
Cumberland Cres. GL51 9 G2
Cumming Ct. GL52 7 F2

Daffodil St. GL50 10 B1
Dagmar Rd. GL50 10 A2
Dark La. GL51 5 H2
Dart Rd. GL52 7 F4
Darwin Clo. GL51 8 D3
Davallia Dri. GL51 9 G6
David French Ct. GL51 9 G6
Daylesford Clo. GL51 9 G4
Deacon Clo. GL51 9 G4
Deakin Clo. GL51 5 H2
Deans Ct. GL51 9 G4
Deep St. GL52 7 G3
Deferriers Walk. GL51 5 E6
Denbigh Rd. GL51 9 F5
Derwent Way. GL51 9 F4
Detmore Clo. GL53 11 H4
Devon Av. GL51 9 G2
Devonshire St. GL50 12 A1
Dill Av. GL51 5 F5
Dinas Clo. GL51 9 F5
Dinas Rd. GL51 9 F5
Distel Clo. GL50 6 A2
Dog Bark La. GL51 5 F1
Dormer Rd. GL51 5 G5
Dorrincourt Mws. GL50 6 A5
Dorrington Walk. GL51 5 E6
Dorset Av. GL51 9 G1
Douro Rd. GL50 6 A6
Doverhay. GL51 9 F5
Dowty Rd. GL51 9 F1
Drakes Pl. GL50 6 A6
Draycott Rd. GL51 9 F3
Drayton Clo. GL51 6 A1
Duckworth Clo. GL53 10 B4
Duke St. GL52 6 D6
Dumbleton Gro. GL51 8 C5
Dunalley Par. GL50 6 C4
Dunalley St. GL50 12 C1
Dunbar Clo. GL51 4 D5
Dunster Gdns. GL51 5 E6
Dunster Gro. GL51 4 D6
Dunster Rd. GL51 4 D6
Durham Clo. GL51 9 G6

East Approach Dri. GL52 6 D3
East Court Villa. GL52 11 G3
East End Rd. GL53 11 G3
Eaton Pl. GL53 12 C5
Edendale App. GL51 8 D3
Edendale Rd. GL51 8 D3
Edinburgh Pl. GL51 9 F1
Edward St. GL50 10 B2
Eldon Av. GL52 7 E6
Eldon Rd. GL52 7 E5
Eldorado Cres. GL50 9 H2
Eldorado Rd. GL50 9 H2
Ellesmere Gro. GL51 9 H5
Elliot Pl. GL51 9 G4
Ellison Rd. GL51 5 F6
Elm Clo,
Prestbury. GL52 7 F2
Elm Clo,
St Peters. GL51 6 A3
Elm Garden Dri. GL51 8 B3
Elm St. GL51 6 A3
Elmfield Av. GL51 6 B3
Elmfield Rd. GL51 6 B3
Emperor Clo. GL51 9 E1
Ennerdale Rd. GL51 9 F4
Enterprise Way. GL51 5 H6
Essex Av. GL51 9 H1
Ettington Clo. GL51 4 D6
Evelyn Clo. GL53 10 D4
Evenlode Rd. GL52 7 E4
Everest Rd. GL51 10 C5
Evesham Rd. GL52 6 D1
Evington Rd. GL51 9 F1

Ewens Rd. GL52 11 E1
Ewlyn Rd. GL53 10 B3
Exmouth Ct. GL53 10 C2
Exmouth St. GL53 10 C2
Eynon Clo. GL53 10 B3
Fairfield Av. GL53 10 B3
Fairfield Par. GL53 10 C3
Fairfield Park Rd. GL53 10 B3
Fairfield St. GL53 10 B3
Fairfield Walk. GL53 10 C3
Fairhaven Rd. GL53 10 C3
Fairhaven St. GL53 10 C3
Fairmount Rd. GL51 9 G2
Fairview Clo. GL52 6 D5
Fairview Rd. GL52 12 D2
Fairview St. GL52 6 D5
Falkland Pl. GL51 5 E6
Faringdon Rd. GL51 9 E4
Farleigh Clo. GL52 11 G3
Farm Clo. GL51 5 E6
Farm La. GL53 10 A5
Farmfield Rd. GL51 9 G6
Farmington Rd. GL51 9 E3
Fauconberg Rd. GL50 12 A4
Fawley Dri. GL52 7 G3
Ferndales Clo. GL51 9 G6
Fernleigh Cres. GL51 9 E5
Fiddlers Green La. GL51 8 C2
Finchcroft Ct. GL52 7 H3
Finchcroft La. GL52 7 H3
Finstock Clo. GL51 9 F3
Fir Grove Walk. GL51 8 D4
FirTree Clo. GL52 7 F3
Fisher Walk. GL51 5 G4
Fleckers Dri. GL51 9 G4
Flint Rd. GL51 9 E5
Florida Dri. GL52 7 G3
Folly La. GL50 6 B3
Fortina Clo. GL50 6 B1
Foxgrove Dri. GL52 7 F6
Frampton Mews. GL51 8 A4
Francis St. GL53 10 B2
Frank Brookes Rd. GL51 5 G4
Frewin Clo. GL51 9 E1
Friars Clo. GL51 9 H6
*Fulbrook Clo,
  Pilgrove Way. GL51 5 E4

Gadshill Rd. GL53 11 F6
Gallops La. GL52 7 H3
Garden Rd. GL53 11 F5
Gardeners La. GL51 6 A3
Gardenia Gro. GL51 9 G6
Genista Way. GL51 9 G6
George Readings Way.
  GL51 5 E6
Giffard Way. GL53 10 C5
Gladstone Rd. GL53 11 F4
Glamorgan Rd. GL51 9 E5
Glebe Farm Ct. GL51 9 F6
Glebe Rd. GL52 7 F3
Glencairn Clo. GL50 9 G3
Glencairn Pk Rd. GL50 9 G3
Glenfall St. GL52 6 D5
Glenfall Way. GL52 11 F3
Glenlea Gro. GL51 9 F6
Glensanda Ct. GL50 12 B6
Gloucester Pl. GL52 12 D3
Gloucester Rd. GL51 8 D3
Glynbridge Gdns. GL51 5 G4
Glyndthorpe Gro. GL51 9 F6
Glynrosa Rd. GL53 11 F4
Godfrey Clo. GL51 9 G4
Golden Miller Rd. GL50 6 B2
Golden Valley
  Bypass. GL51 8 A4
Goldsmith Rd. GL51 9 F1
Goodwin Clo. GL52 7 E5
Gordon Rd. GL53 10 B4
Grace Gdns. GL51 8 D4
Grafton Rd. GL50 10 B2
Graham Pl. GL51 5 E6
Grange Walk. GL51 11 F4
Granley Clo. GL51 9 F3
Granley Dri. GL51 9 G3
Granley Rd. GL51 9 F3
Granville St. GL50 6 B4
Grasmere Rd. GL51 9 F4
Gratton Rd. GL50 10 B2
Gratton St. GL50 10 B2
Gravel Pit La. GL52 7 H2
Graveney St. GL51 5 E4
Great Norwood St. GL50 10 B2
Great Western Rd. GL50 6 B5
Great WesternTer. GL50 6 A5
Greatfield Dri. GL53 10 D4

Greatfield La. GL51 9 F6
Greenhills Clo. GL53 10 D4
Greenhills Rd. GL53 10 D4
Greenway La. GL52 7 G6
Grenadier Rd. GL51 5 F4
Grevil Rd. GL51 5 G5
Greville Ct. GL51 9 F3
Griffiths Av. GL51 9 G3
Grimwade Clo. GL51 9 G2
Gristmill Clo. GL51 5 E4
Grosvenor Pl Sth.
  GL52 12 D3
Grosvenor St. GL52 12 D3
GrosvenorTer. GL52 12 D3
Grove St. GL50 12 A1
Grovefield Way. GL51 8 C4
Grovelands Clo. GL51 11 F3
Gwernant Rd. GL51 9 F5

Hales Clo. GL51 7 E5
Hales Rd. GL52 7 E6
Hall Rd. GL53 10 B5
Halland Rd. GL51 10 B4
Hallmead Clo. GL51 5 E4
Ham Clo. GL52 11 G2
Ham Rd. GL52 11 G2
Ham Sq. GL52 11 H2
Hambrook St. GL52 11 F2
Hamilton St. GL53 11 F2
Hamlet Clo. GL51 9 F1
Hammond Ct. GL53 10 C2
Hampton Clo. GL51 9 H6
Hannam Clo. GL53 10 C5
*Hanover Ct, St Stephens
  Rd. GL51 10 A2
Hanover St. GL50 6 C4
Harp Hill. GL52 7 F5
Harrington Dri. GL51 9 F4
Hartbury Clo. GL51 4 D6
Hartlebury Way. GL52 11 G3
Hartley Clo. GL53 10 D5
Harvest Gro. GL51 5 E4
Haslette Way. GL51 9 F6
Hatherley Brake. GL51 9 E4
Hatherley Court Rd. GL51 9 H4
Hatherley Gate. GL51 9 H4
Hatherley La. GL51 8 D3
Hatherley Rd. GL51 9 E5
Hatherley St. GL50 10 A2
Hawcombe Mews. GL51 9 F6
Haweswater Rd. GL51 9 F5
Hawkswood Rd. GL51 9 F6
Hawthorn Rd. GL51 5 F6
Hayden La. GL51 4 B5
Hayden Rd. GL51 5 F4
Hayes Rd. GL51 7 E5
Hayscotts. GL53 10 C3
Haywards La. GL52 11 E1
Haywards Rd. GL52 11 E2
Hazebrouk Clo. GL51 9 F4
Hazelwood Clo. GL51 9 H6
Hazle Dean Rd. GL51 4 D4
Hazlit Croft. GL51 5 E5
Heapey Clo. GL51 9 E1
Hearne Clo. GL53 11 G3
Hearne Rd. GL53 11 F3
Helens Clo. GL51 5 E5
Hendre Mws. GL50 6 A5
Henley Rd. GL51 4 D6
Henrietta St. GL50 12 B2
Hereford Pl. GL50 6 B4
Hermitage St. GL53 10 B2
Heron Clo. GL51 9 F4
Hesters Way La. GL51 5 E5
Hesters Way Rd. GL51 5 E6
Hetton Gdns. GL53 11 F2
Hewlett Pl. GL52 6 D6
Hewlett Rd. GL52 6 D6
Hicks Beach Rd. GL51 5 E6
High St,
  Cheltenham. GL50 12 A1
High St,
  Prestbury. GL52 7 G2
Highbury La. GL52 12 D3
Highland Rd. GL51 10 D5
Highwood Av. GL53 10 A3
Hill Top Rd. GL50 6 C2
Hill View Rd. GL52 7 F5
Hillands Dri. GL53 10 C5
Hillary Rd. GL53 10 C5
Hillcourt Rd. GL52 6 D2
Hillfield. GL51 9 G2
Hillier Dri. GL51 9 G6
Hillside Clo. GL51 9 G4
Hine Gdns. GL52 7 E4
Hobby Clo. GL53 10 B4
Hollis Gdns. GL51 8 D5

Hollis Rd. GL51 8 D5
Holmer Cres. GL51 9 E5
Home Clo. GL51 5 F5
Home Farm Ct. GL52 11 F2
Homecroft Dri. GL51 5 E3
Honeybourne Dri. GL51 5 E4
Honeysuckle Clo. GL52 7 G4
Hope St. GL51 6 A3
Hopwood Gro. GL52 7 E5
Horsefair St. GL53 11 E3
Howell Rd. GL51 5 F4
Hudson St. GL50 6 B3
Hulbert Clo. GL51 5 H2
Hulbert Cres. GL51 9 F6
Humber Rd. GL52 7 F5
Hungerford St. GL50 6 C4
Huntscote Rd. GL51 5 H3
Huntsfield Clo. GL50 6 D3

Imjin Rd. GL52 7 F5
Imperial Circus. GL50 12 C3
Imperial La. GL50 12 B4
Imperial Sq. GL50 12 B4
INDUSTRIAL & RETAIL:
Arle Ind Est. GL51 5 H4
Battledown
  Trading Est. GL52 11 E1
Charlton Kings
  Ind Est. GL53 11 E5
Cheltenham
  Trading Pk. GL51 5 H6
Gallagher Retail Pk.
  GL51 5 G3
Kingsditch
  Retail Pk. GL51 5 G4
Lansdown Ind Est.
  GL51 9 G2
Manchester Park
  Ind Est. GL51 5 H5
St Johns
  Business Pk. GL51 9 H1
Shaftsbury
  Ind Est. GL51 5 H3
Inkerman La. GL50 10 A2
Isbourne Rd. GL52 7 F5
Ismay Rd. GL51 5 F5
Ivy Bank. GL52 7 G3

Jacobs Ladder. GL52 11 F1
Japonica Dri. GL51 9 G6
Jasmin Way. GL51 9 G6
Jenner Gdns. GL52 12 B2
Jenner Walk. GL52 12 B2
Jersey Av. GL52 7 E5
Jersey St. GL52 6 D5
Jessop Av. GL50 12 A2
Joyner Rd. GL51 5 G4
Juniper Ct. GL51 8 D1
Justica Way. GL51 9 G6

Keire Walk. GL51 5 G4
Kemble Gro. GL51 8 C4
Kemerton Rd. GL51 9 H5
Kempton Gro. GL51 8 D1
Kenelm Dri. GL53 10 B3
Kenelm Gdns. GL53 10 A3
Kenneth Clo. GL51 10 C5
Kensington Av. GL50 9 H3
Kentmere Clo. GL51 9 F4
Kerstin Clo. GL50 6 B2
Kestrel Clo. GL53 10 B4
Keswick Rd. GL51 9 F4
Kew Pl. GL53 10 C2
Keynsham Bank. GL52 10 D1
Keynsham Rd. GL52 10 D2
Keynsham St. GL52 10 D1
Keynshambury Rd.
  GL52 10 D1
Kidnappers La. GL53 10 A5
Kimberley Walk. GL52 7 G5
King Alfred Way. GL51 11 E1
King Arthur Clo. GL51 11 E2
King George Clo. GL53 10 D3
King Henry Clo. GL53 10 D3
King James Clo. GL53 10 D3
King William Dri. GL53 10 D3
Kings Rd. GL52 7 E6
Kingscote Av. GL51 9 E4
Kingscote Clo. GL51 9 E4
Kingscote Gro. GL51 9 E4
Kingscote Rd E. GL51 9 E4
Kingscote Rd W. GL51 9 E4
Kingsditch La. GL51 5 H4
Kingsley Gdns. GL51 9 F2
Kingsmead Av. GL51 5 F5
Kingsmead Clo. GL51 5 G5
Kingsmead Rd. GL51 5 G5

Kingston Dri. GL51 8 D2
Kingsville Rd. GL51 5 H4
Kipling Rd. GL51 9 F2
Knapp La. GL50 12 A2
Knapp Rd. GL50 12 A2
Knightsbridge Cres. GL53 11 E2

Laburnum Ct. GL51 8 D1
Ladysmith Rd. GL52 7 G4
Lake St. GL52 7 F2
Landor Gdns. GL52 7 E5
Langdale Rd. GL51 9 G4
Langdon Rd. GL53 10 B3
Langton Grove Rd. GL52 11 E2
Langton Pl. GL53 11 E2
Lansdown Castle Dri.
  GL51 9 G3
Lansdown Clo. GL51 9 G3
Lansdown Cres. GL50 10 A1
Lansdown Cres La.
  GL50 10 A1
Lansdown Lodge Dri.
  GL51 9 H3
Lansdown Par. GL50 10 A1
Lansdown Pl. GL50 10 A1
Lansdown Pl La. GL50 10 A1
Lansdown Rd. GL51 9 G3
Lansdown Ter La. GL50 6 B6
Lansdown Walk. GL50 10 A1
Larch Clo. GL53 11 G4
Larchmere Gro. GL51 9 F6
Larput Pl. GL50 6 C4
Laurel Dri. GL52 7 F3
Lavender Rd. GL51 9 G6
Lawrence Clo. GL52 11 G3
Lawson Glade. GL53 11 E4
Laxton Rd. GL51 9 F1
Laxton Walk. GL51 9 F1
Lechmere Rd. GL51 5 F6
Leckhampton Farm Ct.
  GL51 10 A5
Leckhampton La. GL51 10 A6
Leckhampton Pl. GL53 10 C4
Leckhampton Rd. GL53 10 B3
Ledmore Rd. GL53 11 F3
Lee Clo. GL51 5 G5
Leighton Rd. GL52 6 D6
Leinster Clo. GL51 4 D5
Lewis Rd. GL51 9 E1
Leyson Rd. GL51 8 C4
Libertus Ct. GGL51 9 G2
Libertus Rd. GL51 9 G2
Lichfield Dri. GL51 9 H6
Liddington Clo. GL53 10 C5
Liddington Rd. GL53 10 C5
Lilac Clo. GL51 9 G6
Limber Hill. GL50 6 B2
Lime Clo. GL52 7 E2
Lincoln Dri. GL51 9 G6
Linden Av. GL51 7 E2
Linden Clo. GL52 7 F2
Linton Ct. GL53 10 C2
Linwell Clo. GL51 6 A2
Lipson Rd. GL51 5 F5
Little Bayshill Ter. GL50 12 A3
Little Cleevemount. GL52 6 D3
Little Herberts Clo. GL53 11 F4
Little Herberts Rd. GL53 11 F4
Littledown Rd. GL50 10 D5
London Rd. GL52 11 E2
Long Mynd Av. GL51 9 E5
Longway Av. GL53 11 E5
Lower Mill St. GL51 6 A4
Loweswater Clo. GL51 9 G4
Loweswater Rd. GL51 9 G4
Lyfield Clo. GL53 11 F3
Lyfield Rd East. GL53 11 F3
Lyfield Rd West. GL53 11 E3
Lygon Walk. GL51 5 G5
Lyndale Ter. GL51 9 H1
Lynworth Pl. GL52 7 F4
Lypiatt Dri. GL50 10 B1
Lypiatt Rd. GL50 10 B1
Lypiatt St. GL50 10 A2

Mackenzie Way. GL51 5 G3
Magnolia Ct. GL51 8 D1
Maidavale Rd. GL53 10 C3
Malden Rd. GL52 6 D4
Malmesbury Rd. GL51 5 G4
Malthouse La. GL50 6 C4
Malvern Pl. GL50 6 A6
Malvern Rd. GL50 6 A5
Malvern St. GL51 6 A3
Mandarin Way. GL50 6 A1
Manor Ct. GL51 5 H2
Manor Pk. GL51 9 E5
Manor Rd. GL51 5 G4

Manse Gdns. GL51
Manser St. GL50
Maple Dri. GL53
Marchant Clo. GL51
Margrett Rd. GL50
Market St. GL50
Marle Hill Par. GL50
Marle Hill Rd. GL50
Marsh Clo. GL51
Marsh Dri. GL51
Marsh Gdns. GL51
Marsh La. GL51
Marsland Rd. GL51
Marston Rd. GL52
Maythorn Dri. GL51
Mead Clo. GL53
Mead Rd. GL53
Meadow Clo. GL51
Meadow La. GL51
Medoc Clo. GL50
Melbourne Clo. GL53
Mendip Clo. GL52
Mendip Rd. GL52
Merestones Clo. GL50
Merestones Dri. GL50
Merestones Rd. GL50
Merlin Way. GL53
Merriville Gdns. GL51
Merriville Rd. GL51
Mersey Rd. GL52
Midwinter Av. GL51
Midwinter Clo. GL50
Mill House Dri. GL50
Mill La,
  Charlton Kings. GL54
Mill La,
  Prestbury. GL52
Mill St. GL52
Millbrook Gdns. GL50
Millbrook St. GL50
Milsom St. GL50
Milton Av. GL51
Milton Rd. GL51
Mimosa Av. GL51
Miserden Rd. GL51
Mitre St. GL53
Monica Dri. GL51
Monkscroft. GL51
Monson Av. GL50
Montgomery Rd. GL51
Montpellier Arc. GL50
Montpellier Av. GL50
Montpellier Dri. GL50
Montpellier Gro. GL50
Montpellier Par. GL50
Montpellier Spa Rd.
  GL50
Montpellier St. GL50
Montpellier Ter. GL50
Montpellier Villas. GL50
Montpellier Walk. GL50
Moor Court Dri. GL52
Moorend Cres. GL53
Moorend Glade. GL53
Moorend Gro. GL53
Moorend Park Rd. GL53
Moorend Rd,
  Charlton Kings. GL53
Moorend Rd,
  Leckhampton. GL53
Moorend St. GL53
Moors Av. GL51
Morlands Dri. GL53
Morningside Ct. GL52
Morningside Ct Yd. GL52
Mornington Dri. GL53
Morris Ct. GL51
Morris Hill Clo. GL51
Mulberry Ct. GL51
Murvagh Clo. GL53
Muscroft Rd. GL52

Naunton Cres. GL53
Naunton Par..GL53
Naunton Pk Clo. GL53
Naunton Pk Rd. GL53
Naunton Ter. GL53
Naunton Way. GL53
Nelmes Row. GL52
Netherwood Gdns. GL51
Nettleton Rd. GL51
New Barn Av. GL51
New Barn Clo. GL51
New Rutland Ct. GL50
New St. GL50

t. GL53 | 11 F4
urt Pk. GL53 | 11 E3
urt Rd. GL53 | 11 E3
n Clo. GL51 | 9 F1
n Rd. GL51 | 5 F6
k Av. GL51 | 9 G2
l Ter. GL50 | 12 B1
Hall Mews. GL52 | 7 E5
Pl. GL50 | 12 C2
Rd East. GL51 | 8 C4
Rd West. GL51 | 8 B4
St. GL50 | 12 C2
ank Clo. GL51 | 8 C4
ield Ter. GL50 | 12 C1
sh Dri. GL51 | 9 G5
od Rd. GL50 | 10 B2
ove Clo. GL51 | 9 F3
e Clo. GL53 | 10 A5
on Av. GL52 | 7 H3
on La. GL52 | 7 H3
Clo. GL51 | 8 D2

r. GL52 | 11 E2
anor Dri. GL52 | 7 E5
ook Dri. GL51 | 8 D4
d St. GL50 | 10 A2
rst Rise. GL50 | 11 F1
d Av. GL52 | 7 E3
d St. GL53 | 11 E2
Rd. GL52 | 7 F6
Rd. GL51 | 5 G4
d. GL53 | 11 F4
th Rd. GL53 | 10 D2
ucester Rd. GL51 | 4 A6
llbrook Ter. GL50 | 6 A5
ddings Clo. GL51 | 8 D4
ddings Rd. GL51 | 8 D4
ation Dri. GL53 | 10 C4
y Clo. GL51 | 5 E6
y Rd. GL51 | 5 E6
d Cres. GL51 | 9 F3
a. GL53 | 12 C6
d Av. GL51 | 5 F6
rd Pl.
ndon Rd. GL52 | 12 B1
d Way. GL51 | 5 F5
d. GL50 | 12 C4
d Pl. GL50 | 12 B3
d Ter. GL50 | 12 B4
ale Ter. GL53 | 12 D6
r Rd. GL53 | 10 B4
e Clo. GL51 | 9 F1
ook Dri. GL52 | 7 E3
ury St. GL53 | 11 F2
n Park Rd. GL50 | 6 B5
n Rd. GL50 | 6 A6
Clo. GL52 | 6 D6
Par. GL52 | 6 D6
Passage. GL50 | 12 C2
t St.GL52 | 6 D6
Way. GL51 | 9 G6

cks La. GL50 | 6 C2
rick Rd. GL50 | 10 B3
la Clo. GL50 | 12 A4
la La. GL50 | 12 A4
la Rd. GL50 | 12 A4
n Ter. GL53 | 12 C6
ate. GL50 | 10 B2
. GL52 | 7 F1
ews. GL53 | 10 A3
. GL50 | 10 B2
. GL50 | 6 B5
ew. GL51 | 5 E5
ry Clo. GL51 | 9 G1
ad Rd. GL53 | 10 D5
od Gro. GL53 | 11 E5
v. GL51 | 9 H1
ale Clo. GL51 | 5 G4
k Clo. GL51 | 8 D1
o. GL51 | 11 G3
s Ct. GL50 | 10 A1
dge Clo. GL52 | 11 G3
oke Rd. GL51 | 9 E5
Clo. GL50 | 6 A1
va Clo. GL51 | 5 G6
e Rd. GL52 | 7 F3
vania Av. GL51 | 5 F5
Rd. GL51 | 9 F4
nlon Way. GL50 | 6 B4
ne Rd. GL53 | 10 B4
ennel Clo. GL51 | 5 E4
nt La. GL51 | 8 B2
lly Way. GL52 | 7 H3
g Clo. GL53 | 10 B3
g Rd. GL53 | 10 B3
Av. GL53 | 10 D5

Pilford Clo. GL53 | 10 D4
Pilford Ct. GL53 | 10 C6
Pilford Rd. GL53 | 10 C6
*Pilgrove Clo,
  Pilgrove Way. GL53 | 5 E4
Pilgrove Way. GL53 | 5 E4
Pilley Cres. GL53 | 10 C5
Pilley La. GL53 | 10 C5
Pine Clo. GL52 | 11 E1
Pinetrees. GL53 | 11 E3
Pitman Rd. GL51 | 9 E2
Pittville Circus. GL52 | 6 D4
Pittville Circus Rd. GL52 | 7 E5
Pittville Ct. GL52 | 6 D3
Pittville Cres. GL52 | 6 D4
Pittville Cres Lane. GL52 | 6 D4
Pittville Lawn. GL52 | 6 D4
Pittville Mews. GL52 | 12 D1
Pittville St. GL52 | 12 C3
Polefield Gdns. GL51 | 9 H3
Poole Way. GL50 | 6 B4
Popes Clo. GL50 | 6 B4
Portland Sq. GL52 | 6 D5
Portland St. GL52 | 12 C2
Porturet Way. GL53 | 11 F3
Post Office La. GL50 | 12 B3
Postlip Way. GL51 | 9 E3
Prescott Walk. GL52 | 7 F3
Prestbury Green Dri.
  GL52 | 7 G3
Prestbury Rd. GL52 | 7 E4
Prince's Ct. GL50 | 10 A2
Prince's Rd. GL50 | 10 A2
Princess St. GL52 | 7 E6
Princess Elizabeth Way.
  GL51 | 5 F6
Priors Rd. GL52 | 7 F5
Priory Pl. GL52 | 10 D1
Priory St. GL52 | 6 D6
Priory Ter. GL52 | 6 D6
Priory Walk. GL52 | 6 D6
Promenade. GL50 | 12 B4
Prospect Ter. GL52 | 6 D5
Pumphreys Rd. GL53 | 11 F3
Purbeck Way. GL52 | 7 G3
Pyrton Mews. GL51 | 9 E6

Quat Goose La. GL51 | 5 H1
Queen St. GL51 | 6 A4
Queens Circus. GL50 | 12 A5
Queens Ct. GL51 | 9 H3
Queens La. GL50 | 10 B1
Queens Par. GL50 | 10 B1
Queens Retreat. GL51 | 6 A5
Queens Rd. GL50 | 9 H2
Queenwood Gro. GL52 | 7 H2

Radnor Rd. GL51 | 9 F5
Randolf Clo. GL51 | 11 E3
Ravensgate Rd. GL53 | 11 F5
Reaburn Clo. GL52 | 11 G3
Red Rower Clo. GL50 | 6 B1
Redding Rd. GL51 | 8 D4
Reddings Pk. GL51 | 8 D4
Redgrove Park. GL51 | 9 E4
Redgrove Rd. GL51 | 5 G5
Redthorne Way. GL51 | 9 F6
Redwood Ct. GL51 | 8 D1
Regent Arcade. GL50 | 12 C3
*Regent Ct, St
  Stephens Rd. GL50 | 10 A2
Regent St. GL50 | 12 C3
Regis Clo. GL53 | 11 E4
Richards Rd. GL51 | 6 A3
Richmond Dri. GL52 | 7 F5
Rippledale Clo. GL51 | 9 E4
Rissington Clo. GL51 | 9 F3
Rivelands Rd. GL51 | 5 H2
Rivers Leys. GL51 | 5 H4
Riverside Clo. GL52 | 11 G3
Riverview Way. GL51 | 5 G4
Robert Burns Av. GL51 | 9 E4
Roberts Rd. GL52 | 7 H4
Robins Clo. GL52 | 7 E4
Rochester Clo. GL51 | 9 H6
Rodney Rd. GL50 | 12 C4
Rolleston Way. GL51 | 9 F4
Roman Hackle Av. GL50 | 6 B2
Roman Hackle Rd. GL50 | 6 B2
Roman Rd. GL51 | 9 G2
Roosevelt Av. GL52 | 11 E1
Rope Walk. GL52 | 12 B1
Rose and Crown
  Passage. GL50 | 12 C2
Rosehill St. GL52 | 11 E1
Rothermere Clo. GL51 | 9 G6
Rothleigh. GL52 | 9 F6

Rotunda Ter. GL50 | 12 A5
Rowan Way. GL51 | 9 F6
Rowanfield Rd. GL51 | 9 G2
Roxton Dri. GL51 | 8 C4
Royal Cres. GL50 | 12 B3
Royal Oak Mews. GL50 | 12 A1
Royal Par Mews. GL50 | 12 A5
Royal Well La. GL50 | 12 A3
Royal Well Pl. GL50 | 12 A3
Royal Well Rd. GL50 | 12 B4
Runnings Rd. GL51 | 5 G3
Runnymede. GL51 | 9 E6
Rushworth Clo. GL51 | 8 D1
Rushy Mws. GL52 | 7 F3
Russell Pl. GL51 | 6 B4
Russell St. GL51 | 6 B4
Russett Rd. GL51 | 5 F5
Rutherford Way. GL51 | 5 G4
Rydal Walk. GL51 | 9 F4
Rye Av. GL51 | 5 E4
Ryeworth Dri. GL52 | 11 G2
Ryeworth Rd. GL52 | 11 F2

Sackville App. GL50 | 6 C3
*Saddlers La,
  Tivoli Wk. GL50 | 10 A2
Sadlers Ct. GL53 | 10 D1
St Aidans Clo. GL51 | 9 E1
St Albans Clo. GL51 | 9 H6
St Annes Clo. GL52 | 6 D5
St Annes Rd. GL52 | 6 D6
St Annes Ter. GL52 | 6 D5
St Arvans Ct. GL52 | 6 D3
St Davids Clo. GL51 | 9 G5
St Edwards Walk. GL53 | 11 E2
St Georges Clo. GL51 | 6 A5
St Georges Dri. GL51 | 6 A5
St Georges Pl. GL50 | 12 A3
St Georges Rd. GL50 | 12 A3
St Georges Sq. GL50 | 12 B2
St Georges St. GL50 | 12 B1
St Georges Ter. GL50 | 12 A3
St James Pl. GL50 | 10 B2
St James Sq. GL50 | 10 B1
St James's St. GL52 | 6 D6
St Johns Av. GL52 | 6 D6
St Judes Walk. GL53 | 11 E2
St Lukes Pl. GL53 | 12 C5
St Lukes Rd. GL53 | 12 C5
St Margarets Rd. GL50 | 12 C1
St Margarets Ter. GL50 | 12 C1
St Michaels Rd. GL51 | 9 H6
St Nicholas Dri. GL50 | 6 C2
St Pauls La. GL50 | 6 B4
St Pauls Rd. GL50 | 6 B4
St Pauls St Nth. GL50 | 6 C4
St Pauls St Sth. GL50 | 12 B1
St Peters Clo. GL51 | 5 H5
St Peters Sq. GL51 | 5 H5
St Phillips St. GL50 | 10 B2
St Stephens Clo. GL51 | 10 A2
St Stephens Manor.
  GL51 | 10 A2
St Stephens Rd. GL51 | 10 A2
Salamanca. GL52 | 7 G5
Salisbury Av. GL51 | 9 G5
Salix Ct. GL51 | 9 G6
Sandford Mill Clo.
  GL53 | 10 D2
Sandford Mill Rd.
  GL53 | 10 D2
Sandford Rd. GL53 | 10 C1
Sandford St. GL53 | 12 C5
Sandhurst Rd. GL52 | 11 F3
Sandy La. GL52 | 10 D4
Sandy La Rd. GL53 | 11 E4
Sappercombe La. GL53 | 11 F4
Saville Clo. GL50 | 6 D3
Saxon Way. GL52 | 11 E1
School Rd. GL53 | 11 F3
Seabright Clo. GL51 | 5 F4
Seacombe Rd. GL51 | 9 E1
Sedgewick Gdns. GL51 | 9 E5
Sefton Wk. GL51 | 9 F6
Selkirk Clo. GL52 | 6 D4
Selkirk Gdns. GL52 | 6 D4
Selkirk St. GL52 | 6 D4
Selworthy. GL51 | 9 F6
Seneca Way. GL53 | 10 A2
Sevelm. GL51 | 9 F6
Seven Posts All. GL52 | 7 F3
Severn Rd. GL51 | 7 E4
Shakespeare Rd. GL51 | 9 E3
Shaw Green La. GL51 | 7 F1
Sheepscombe Clo. GL51 | 9 E3
Shelburne Rd. GL51 | 9 G4
Sheldons Ct. GL52 | 12 D2
Shelley Av. GL51 | 9 F2

Shelley Rd. GL51 | 9 E2
Shepherds Clo. GL51 | 5 E4
Sherborne Pl. GL52 | 6 D5
Sherborne St. GL52 | 6 D5
Short St. GL53 | 10 B3
Shrublands. GL53 | 11 E4
Shurdington Rd. GL53 | 10 A4
Sidney St. GL52 | 6 D6
Silverthorne Clo. GL51 | 10 A4
Silverwood Way. GL51 | 9 F5
Sissinghurst Gro. GL51 | 9 G6
Skillicorne Mews. GL50 | 9 H3
Smithwood Gro. GL53 | 11 E5
Smythe Rd. GL51 | 5 H2
Solway Rd. GL51 | 4 D5
Somergate Rd. GL51 | 5 E4
Somerset Av. GL51 | 9 G1
Somerset Pass. GL50 | 12 A3
Somme Rd. GL52 | 7 F4
South View Way. GL52 | 7 G3
Southam Rd. GL52 | 7 G1
Southcourt Clo. GL53 | 10 C4
Southcourt Dri. GL53 | 10 C4
Southern Rd. GL53 | 10 C5
Southfield App. GL53 | 10 D5
Southfield Clo. GL53 | 10 D5
Southfield Rise. GL53 | 10 D5
Southgate Dri. GL53 | 10 D2
Southwood La. GL50 | 10 B1
Spenser Av. GL51 | 9 F2
Spenser Rd. GL51 | 9 F2
Spring La. GL52 | 7 F1
Springbank Dri. GL51 | 4 D6
Springbank Gro. GL51 | 4 D6
Springbank Rd. GL51 | 4 D6
Springbank Way. GL51 | 5 E5
Springfield Clo. GL51 | 8 C4
Stancombe Gro. GL51 | 9 G6
Stanley Pl. GL51 | 5 E6
Stanley Rd. GL52 | 7 F6
Stanton Way. GL51 | 9 F3
Stantons Dri. GL51 | 5 H2
Stanway Rd. GL51 | 9 E3
Stanwick Cres. GL51 | 6 A2
Stanwick Dri. GL51 | 6 A2
Stanwick Gdns. GL51 | 6 A3
Station St. GL50 | 12 A2
Stirling Ct. GL51 | 6 A4
Stockton Clo. GL53 | 11 E4
Stoneleigh Clo. GL53 | 10 C6
Stoneville St. GL51 | 6 B4
Stow Ct. GL51 | 9 H2
Strickland Rd. GL52 | 11 E1
Studland Rd. GL52 | 7 G3
Suffolk Par. GL50 | 10 B1
Suffolk Rd. GL50 | 10 B1
Suffolk Sq. GL50 | 10 B1
Suffolk St. GL50 | 10 B2
Summerfield Clo. GL51 | 5 G4
Sun St. GL51 | 6 A4
Sunnyfield La. GL51 | 8 D6
Surrey Av. GL51 | 9 G1
Sussex Av. GL51 | 9 G1
Swallowtail Clo. GL51 | 9 E1
Swanscombe Pl. GL51 | 9 F6
Swanswell Dri. GL51 | 9 F3
Swindon Clo. GL51 | 6 B4
Swindon La. GL50 | 12 A1
Swindon Rd. GL51 | 6 B4
Sycamore Ct. GL51 | 8 D1
Sydenham Rd Nth.
  GL52 | 7 E6
Sydenham Rd Sth.
  GL52 | 7 E6
Sydenham Villas Rd.
  GL52 | 6 D6

Talbot Rd. GL51 | 9 H3
Tamar Rd. GL52 | 7 E4
Tanners La. GL53 | 5 F5
Tanners Rd. GL51 | 5 F6
Tatchley La. GL52 | 7 F3
Tayberry Gro. GL51 | 9 G6
Taylors End. GL50 | 9 H5
Teme Rd. GL52 | 7 E5
Tennyson Rd. GL51 | 9 F2
Tensing Rd. GL53 | 10 D5
Terry Ruck Clo. GL51 | 9 E1
Tewkesbury Rd. GL51 | 4 B1
Thames Rd. GL52 | 7 E4
The Alders. GL51 | 10 A5
The Avenue. GL53 | 10 D4
The Bank. GL52 | 7 G2
The Bramery. GL51 | 9 H1
The Burgage. GL52 | 7 F2
The Close. GL53 | 10 B5

The Conifers. GL52 | 7 E4
The Courtyard. GL50 | 12 A5
The Gardens. GL50 | 6 D3
The Greenings. GL51 | 9 F6
The Grove,
  Christchurch Rd. GL50 | 9 H3
The Grove,
  Hales Rd. GL52 | 7 E6
The Gryphons. GL52 | 7 E5
The Haver. GL52 | 11 F2
The Hawthornes. GL51 | 9 E5
The Lanes. GL51 | 10 A5
The Oaks. GL51 | 8 D5
The Park. GL50 | 10 A3
The Pavilions. GL53 | 12 C6
The Reddings. GL51 | 8 B5
The Runnings. GL51 | 5 H3
The Spindles. GL51 | 10 A5
The Spinney. GL52 | 6 D2
The Stables. GL52 | 7 H2
The Strand. GL50 | 12 D4
The Verneys. GL53 | 10 D3
The Vineyards. GL51 | 9 H2
Thirlestaine Rd. GL53 | 10 C2
Thirlmere Rd. GL51 | 9 F4
Thistledown Clo. GL51 | 5 E4
Thomond Clo. GL50 | 6 A2
Thompson Dri. GL53 | 11 F4
Thornbury Clo. GL51 | 9 H1
Thorncliffe Dri. GL51 | 9 H3
Thornhaugh Mews. GL51 | 9 E6
Three Sisters La. GL52 | 7 H3
Tibberton Gro. GL51 | 8 C4
Tilney Rd. GL51 | 6 C2
Timbercombe La. GL53 | 11 F6
Timbercombe Mews.
  GL53 | 11 F5
Timperley Way. GL51 | 9 E6
Tiverton Clo. GL51 | 4 D6
Tivoli Rd. GL50 | 10 A2
Tivoli St. GL50 | 10 A2
Tivoli Walk. GL50 | 10 A2
Tom Price Clo. GL52 | 6 D5
Tommy Taylors La. GL50 | 6 B3
Townsend St. GL51 | 6 B4
Trafalgar St. GL50 | 10 B1
Treelands Clo. GL53 | 10 C4
Treelands Dri. GL53 | 10 C4
Trelawn Ct. GL50 | 10 B1
Trinity La. GL52 | 12 D2
Trinity School La. GL51 | 6 D5
Trowscoed Av. GL53 | 10 C3
Tryes Rd. GL50 | 10 B3
Tudor Lodge Dri. GL50 | 10 B1
Tudor Lodge Rd. GL50 | 10 B1
Turkdean Rd. GL51 | 9 F3
Tylea Clo. GL53 | 8 D4
Tyler Ct. GL51 | 9 E1

Ullswater Rd. GL51 | 9 F4
Undercliff Av. GL53 | 10 C6
Undercliff Ter. GL51 | 10 C6
Union St. GL52 | 6 D5
Unwin Clo. GL51 | 8 D4
Unwin Rd. GL51 | 8 D4
Up Hatherley Way. GL51 | 8 D5
Upper Bath St. GL50 | 10 B2
Upper Mill La. GL52 | 7 H2
Upper Norwood St.
  GL53 | 10 B3
Upper Park St. GL52 | 11 E1
Upperfield Rd. GL51 | 5 H4

Verney Clo. GL53 | 10 D3
Vernon Pl. GL53 | 12 D4
Viburnum Clo. GL50 | 9 H5
Victoria Pl. GL52 | 6 D6
Victoria Retreat. GL50 | 10 C2
Victoria St. GL50 | 6 B4
Victoria Ter. GL50 | 7 E6
Village Rd. GL51 | 5 F5
Vine Ct. GL50 | 6 B4
Vineries Clo. GL53 | 10 B5
Vineyards Clo. GL53 | 11 F5
Vittoria Walk. GL50 | 12 B5

Waddon Dri. GL52 | 7 E4
Wade Clo. GL51 | 8 D4
Waldrist Clo. GL53 | 5 G4
Walnut Clo. GL52 | 6 D3
Warden Hill Clo. GL51 | 9 F5
Warden Hill Rd. GL51 | 9 F5
Wards Rd. GL51 | 9 E5
Warren Clo. GL51 | 9 G5
Warwick Cres. GL52 | 11 F3
Warwick Pl. GL52 | 12 D2
Wasley Rd. GL51 | 9 E2

31

Water La. GL52 11 F3
Waterfield Clo. GL53 10 C2
Waterloo St. GL51 6 A3
Watermoor Clo. GL51 5 E4
Watershoot Clo. GL52 7 E2
Welch Rd. GL51 5 F5
Well Pl. GL50 6 A6
Well Walk. GL50 12 B2
Welland Ct. GL52 7 E3
Welland Dri. GL52 7 E3
Welland Lodge Rd. GL52 7 E3
Wellesley Rd. GL50 6 C4
Wellington La. GL52 12 D1
Wellington Rd. GL52 6 D4
Wellington Sq. GL50 6 C4
Wellington St. GL50 6 C4
Wells Clo. GL51 9 G6
Welwyn Mews. GL51 9 E6
Wendover Gdns. GL50 9 H2
Wentworth Clo. GL51 5 E6
Wentworth Rd. GL51 5 E6
Wessex Dri. GL52 7 F5
West Approach Dri. GL52 6 D3
West Down Gdns. GL52 6 D5
West Dri. GL50 6 D4
Westal Ct. GL51 9 H4
Westal Grn. GL50 10 A1
Westal Pk. GL51 9 H4
Westbourne Dri. GL52 7 E5
Westbury Rd. GL53 10 C5
Western Rd. GL50 6 A4
Westminster Clo. GL53 11 E2
Westwood La. GL52 7 H4
Whaddon Av. GL52 7 E5
Whaddon Rd. GL52 7 E4
Wheatland Dri. GL51 5 E4
White Cross Sq. GL53 10 C2
White Hart St. GL51 6 B4
Whitemarsh Clo. GL51 5 E4
Whitethorne Dri. GL52 7 G4
Whittington Rd. GL51 9 E3
Whittle Clo. GL51 8 D3
Willersey Rd. GL51 9 E3
William Gough Clo. GL51 5 E4
Willow Rd,
  Battledown. GL52 7 F6
Willow Rd,
  Charlton Kings. GL53 11 G4
Willowbrook Dri. GL51 5 E4
Willowherb Clo. GL52 7 G4
Wimbourne Clo. GL51 9 E5
Winchcombe St. GL52 12 D2
Winchester Way. GL51 9 G5
Windermere Clo. GL51 9 F4
Windermere Rd. GL51 9 F4
Windrush Rd. GL52 7 F5
Windsor St. GL52 6 D4
Windyrldge Gdns. GL50 6 B2
Windyridge Rd. GL50 6 A2
Winstonian Rd. GL52 6 D5
Winterbotham Rd. GL51 5 E6
Winton Clo. GL51 9 G4
Winton Rd. GL51 9 G4
Wisteria Ct. GL51 9 G6
Wistley Rd. GL53 11 G5
Witcombe Pl. GL52 6 D6
Withybridge Gdns. GL51 4 C1
Withybridge La. GL51 4 B4
Withyholt Ct. GL53 11 E4
Withyholt Pk. GL53 11 E4
Withypool. GL51 9 F6
Witley Lodge Clo. GL51 9 F4
Wolseley Ter. GL50 12 C5
Woodgate Clo. GL52 11 H4
Woodlands Rd. GL51 9 H6
Worcester St. GL51 6 A3
Wordsworth Av. GL51 9 E2
Wychbury Clo. GL53 10 B4
Wymans La. GL51 6 A2
Wymans Rd. GL52 7 E4
Yarnold Ter. GL51 5 H5
Yeend Clo. GL51 5 F3
Yew Tree Clo. GL50 6 B2
York Row. GL52 7 F3
York St. GL52 6 D5
York Ter. GL50 12 A3

GLOUCESTER

Abbey Rd. GL2 18 B3
Abbeymead Av. GL4 20 A4
Abbots Rd. GL4 20 B5
Abbotswood Clo. GL4 23 F3
Abbotswood Rd. GL3 26 B2
Acer Gro. GL2 22 A4

Acorn Ct. GL4 24 C2
Adelaide St. GL1 19 E4
Albany St. GL1 19 E4
Albermarle Rd. GL3 17 F4
Albert St. GL1 13 F4
Albion St. GL1 18 C3
Alder Clo. GL2 15 H5
Alders Grn. GL2 15 F4
Alderton Clo. GL4 25 E2
Alexandra Rd. GL1 19 E1
Alfred St. GL1 19 F3
Alington Clo. GL1 19 F3
All Saints Rd. GL1 19 E3
Allendale Clo. GL2 15 H5
Alma Pl. GL1 18 C4
Alma Ter. GL1 18 C4
Almond Clo. GL4 24 D2
Alney Ter. GL1 14 B6
Alpine Clo. GL4 19 G6
Althorp Clo. GL4 22 D4
Alvin St. GL1 13 E1
Amber Clo. GL4 23 E2
Amberley Rd. GL4 24 B1
Anbrook Cres. GL3 20 B4
Andorra Way. GL3 16 D3
Angelica Way. GL4 20 C6
Anne Hathaway Dri.
  GL3 17 H4
Ansdell Dri. GL3 21 G5
Apperley Dri. GL2 22 A5
Apple Tree Clo,
  Abbeymead. GL4 25 E1
Apple Tree Clo,
  Churchdown. GL3 16 C2
Appleton Way. GL3 20 D5
Aragon Way. GL3 16 C2
Archdeacon Ct. GL1 13 B1
Archdeacon St. GL1 13 B2
Archibald St. GL1 19 E3
Ardmore Clo. GL4 23 G3
Argyll Pl. GL2 19 G1
Argyll Rd. GL2 19 G1
Arkendale Dri. GL2 22 A6
Arlingham Rd. GL4 23 F2
Armada Clo. GL3 16 C2
Armscroft Court. GL2 19 G2
Armscroft Cres. GL2 19 G2
Armscroft Gdns. GL2 19 G2
Armscroft Pl. GL2 19 G2
Armscroft Rd. GL2 19 G2
Armscroft Way. GL2 19 G2
Arreton Av. GL4 19 G5
Arrow Head Clo. GL4 24 B2
Arthur St. GL1 19 E3
Arundel Clo. GL4 23 E5
Ascot Ct. GL1 19 F3
Ash Gro. GL4 25 E3
Ash Grove Clo. GL2 22 A6
Ashcroft Clo. GL4 24 D3
Ashgrove Av. GL4 19 H5
Ashgrove Way. GL4 19 H5
Ashleworth Gdns. GL2 22 A5
Ashmead. GL2 15 G4
Ashmore Rd. GL4 23 H1
Ashton Clo. GL4 25 E2
Ashville Rd. GL2 18 B6
Ashwood Way. GL3 20 C5
Askwith Rd. GL4 19 G5
Aspen Dri. GL2 22 A4
Astor Clo. GL3 21 F5
Astridge Rd. GL3 26 D2
Asylum La. GL1 19 F1
Augustine Way. GL4 20 C5
Austin Dri. GL2 15 E3
Avebury Clo. GL4 22 D4
Avening Rd. GL4 19 E6
Avon Cres. GL3 26 C2
Awdry Way. GL4 23 F3
Awebridge Way. GL4 24 C1
Aycote Clo. GL4 19 G6
Ayland Gdns. GL1 19 F3

Bader Av. GL3 17 E4
Badger Clo. GL4 24 D2
Badger Vale Ct. GL2 23 F1
Badminton Rd. GL4 24 B1
Baker St. GL1 18 C3
Balfour Rd. GL1 18 C5
Ballinska Mews. GL4 16 A4
Bamfurlong La. GL51 17 H1
Baneberry Rd. GL4 24 A1
Baptist Clo. GL4 20 C6
Barbican Rd. GL1 13 B3
Barbican Way. GGL1 13 B3
Barley Clo. GL4 26 C3
Barleycroft Clo. GL4 24 D3
Barn Clo. GL4 25 E2

Barnaby Clo. GL1 19 E5
Barnacre Dri. GL3 20 C2
Barnes Wallis Way. GL3 17 E4
Barnfields. GL4 19 E6
Barnett Way. GL4 20 B2
Barnhay. GL3 17 F5
Barnwood Av. GL4 20 A3
Barnwood By-Pass. GL4 20 A2
Barnwood Link Rd.
  GL2 16 B5
Barnwood Rd. GL2 19 G1
Barrack Sq. GL1 13 B3
Barrington Dri. GL3 20 C3
Barrow Clo. GL2 22 B6
Barrow Hill. GL3 17 F6
Barton St. GL1 19 E4
Base La. GL2 14 C1
Basil Clo. GL4 24 D2
Bateman Clo. GL4 23 F4
Bathurst Rd. GL1 19 E5
Bay Tree Rd. GL4 20 C6
Bazeley Rd. GL4 24 B3
Beacon Rd. GL4 24 C3
Bearland. GL1 13 B3
Beaufort Rd. GL4 19 36
Beaumont Rd. GL2 15 H4
Beckford Rd. GL4 25 E2
Beckside Ct. GL1 19 E3
Bedford St. GL1 13 E4
Beech Clo. GL2 22 A6
Beechcroft Rd. GL2 15 F4
Beechwood Gro. GL4 23 G2
Bekdale Clo. GL2 22 A6
Belfry Clo. GL4 20 B4
Belgrave Rd. GL1 19 E3
Belgrave Ter. GL1 19 E4
Bell La. GL1 13 D4
Bell Walk. GL1 13 C3
Belmont Av. GL3 21 E5
Benson Clo. GL4 20 B5
Berkeley St. GL1 13 C3
Berry Lawn. GL4 24 D3
Berryfield Glade. GL3 16 D3
Betjeman Clo. GL3 23 E1
Bewley Way. GL3 16 D3
Bibury Rd. GL4 19 E5
Bijou Ct. GL1 15 E5
Bilberry Clo. GL4 25 F1
Billbrook Rd. GL3 20 D4
Billingham Clo. GL4 19 G5
Birch Av. GL4 19 G5
Birchall Av. GL4 24 C3
Birchmore Rd. GL1 19 F3
Birchwood Fields. GL4 23 G2
Birdwood Clo. GL4 2b E2
Birkeley Clo. GL3 21 E5
Bishopstone Rd. GL1 19 F3
Bisley Rd. GL4 23 G4
Bittern Av. GL4 20 A5
Blaby Clo. GL4 25 F1
Black Dog Way. GL1 13 E2
Blackberry Clo. GL4 25 E1
Blackbird Av. GL3 16 A3
Blackfriars. GL1 13 C3
Blackthorne Gdns. GL2 22 B4
Blackwater Way. GL2 16 A4
Blaisdon Clo. GL4 25 E1
Blake Hill Way. GL4 20 A5
Blakeney Clo. GL4 23 F2
Blenheim Rd. GL1 19 E3
Blinkhorns Bridge La.
  GL2 19 G2
Bloomfield Rd. GL4 18 C5
Bloomfield Ter. GL1 18 C5
Bodiam Av. GL4 22 D3
Boleyn Clo. GL3 16 C2
Bondend Rd. GL4 25 E3
Borage Rd. GL3 20 C6
Bourton Rd. GL4 23 G4
Boverton Av. GL3 21 G6
Boverton Dri. GL3 21 G5
Bowly Rd. GL1 18 C6
Boyce Clo. GL4 25 E2
Bradford Rd. GL2 19 F4
Bradley Clo. GL2 15 G5
Bradshaw Clo. GL2 14 D2
Brae Walk. GL4 24 D2
Braeburn Clo. GL4 19 H1
Bramble Lawn. GL4 24 D3
Bramley Mews. GL4 20 D5
Brandon Clo. GL3 16 D1
Brecon Clo. GL4 22 A5
Breinton Way. GL4 24 D3
Briar Lawn. GL4 24 D3
Briars. GL3 16 D3
Bridge Clo. GL2 18 A5

Bridge Farm. GL2 14 A2
Brierley Clo. GL4 20 B6
Brindle Clo. GL4 24 C1
Brionne Way. GL2 15 G4
Bristol Rd,
  Hardwicke. GL2 26 B4
Bristol Rd,
  Quedgeley. GL2 22 D2
Broad Leys Rd. DL4 20 A4
Broadstone Clo. GL4 20 B3
Broadway. GL4 19 E6
Broadwell Clo. GL4 20 B6
Brockeridge Clo. GL2 22 A4
Brockworth Rd. GL3 21 G1
Brome Rd. GL4 20 C6
Brook St. GL1 18 D4
Brookfield La. GL3 17 G2
Brookfield Rd,
  Churchdown. GL3 17 F5
Brookfield Rd,
  Hucclecote GL3 20 B4
Brooklands Pk. GL2 15 H4
Brookside Villas. GL2 19 G2
Brookthorpe Clo. GL4 23 F3
Brunswick Rd. GL1 13 D4
Brunswick Sq. GL1 18 D3
Bruton Way. GL1 13 E2
Bryerland Rd. GL3 26 D2
Buckholt Way. GL3 26 B2
Buckingham Dri. GL3 16 C2
Buddleia Clo. GL4 25 F1
Bull La. GL1 13 C3
Bullfinch Rd. GL4 19 H5
Bullfinch Way. GL3 16 A2
Burford Mews. GL1 19 F3
Burleigh Croft. GL3 20 C3
Burnet Clo. GL4 24 A1
Burns Av. GL2 23 E2
Buscombe Gdns. GL3 20 E4
Bush Hay. GL3 16 D4
Buttercup Lawn. GL4 24 D3
Buttermilk La. GL3 17 E3
Buttington. GL4 25 F1
Byard Rd. GL2 22 D1
Bybrook Gdns. GL4 23 F4
Bybrook Rd. GL4 23 F5
Byron Av. GL2 23 E2

Caesar Rd. GL2 18 B6
Calderdale. GL4 25 F1
Caledonian Rd. GL4 24 C3
Calspick Way. GL2 16 A4
Camberley Clo. GL3 20 D4
Cambridge St. GL1 13 F4
Camomile Clo. GL4 20 C6
Campbell Clo. GL3 16 B2
Campden Rd. GL4 23 G3
Campion Clo. GL4 24 B1
Canning Rd. GL4 16 B4
Capel Rd. GL4 24 C3
Capital Park. GL2 22 D2
Carisbrooke Rd. GL2 20 D5
Carlton Rd. GL1 18 D6
Carmarthen St. GL1 19 E4
Carne Pl. GL4 19 H2
Carters Orchard. GL2 22 B4
Casey Clo. GL1 19 F2
Castle Cotts. GL3 20 B3
Castle Hill Dri. GL3 26 C2
Castleton Rd. GL4 20 A4
Catkin Clo. GL2 22 B6
Cavendish Av. GL3 17 F4
Cecil Rd. GL1 18 C5
Cedar Rd. GL3 21 F4
Cedarwood Dri. GL4 23 G2
Cellars Rd. GL2 26 B3
Cemetery Rd. GL4 19 F5
Central Rd. GL1 18 D4
Centurian Clo. GL4 20 B5
Chaceley Clo. GL4 20 B6
Chaceley Clo. GL2 22 A5
Chadbournes. GL3 17 E3
Chadwick Clo. GL4 23 F3
Chaffinch Clo. GL3 16 A2
Chalford Rd. GL4 23 G4
Chamwells Av. GL2 15 G5
Chamwells Walk. GL2 15 G5
Chancel Clo. GL4 19 G3
Chandos Dri. GL2 26 B2
Chapel Hay Clo. GL3 17 F5
Chapel Hay La. GL3 17 F5
Chapel Gdns. GL2 26 C3
Charlecote Av. GL4 23 E5
Charles St. GL1 19 E3
Charlock Clo. GL4 24 A1
Charlton Way. GL2 15 H4
Chartwell Clo. GL2 18 A5

Chase La. GL4
Chatcombe Rd. GL4
Chatsworth Av. GL4 24 C1
Chaucer Clo. GL1
Chedworth Rd. GL4
Cheltenham Rd. GL2
Cheltenham Rd East.
  GL3
Chequers Rd. GL4
Cherrington Dri. GL4
Cherry Clo. GL2
Cherry Gdns. GL3
Cherrywood Gdns. GL4
Cherston Ct. GL4
Chervil Clo. GL4
Cheshire Rd. GL3
Chesmann Ct. GL2
Chester Rd. GL4
Chestnut Clo. GL2
Chestnut Rd. GL4
Cheviot Clo. GL2
Cheyney Clo. GL4
Chiltern Rd. GL2
Chislet Way. GL4
Choirs Clo. GL4
Chosen Dri. GL3
Chosen Way. GL3
Church Dri. GL2
Church La,
  Barnwood. GL4
Church La,
  Hardwicke. GL2
Church La,
  Whaddon. GL4
Church Rise. GL2
Church Rd,
  Churchdown. GL3
Longlevens. GL2
Church Rd,
  Maisemore. GL2
Church St. GL1
Church Way. GL4
Churchdown La. GL3
Churchfield Rd. GL4
Churchill Rd. GL1
Churchview. GL4
Cirencester Rd. GL3
Clapham Ct. GL1
Clare St. GL1
Claremont Ct. GL1
Claremont Rd. GL1
Clarence St. GLi
Clarence Walk. GL1
Claridge Clo. GL4
Clarkia Clo. GL3
Claudians Clo. GL4
Clearwater Dri. GL2
Cleeve Rd. GL4
Clegram Rd. GL1
Clement St. GL1
Clevedon Rd. GL1
Clifton Rd. GL1
Clomoney Way. GL2
Clover Dri. GL2
Clover Piece. GL4
Clyde Rd. GL3
Coberley Rd. GL4
Cochran Clo. GL3
Coldray Clo. GL1
Cole Av. GL2
Colebridge Av. GL2
Colerne Rd. GL3
Colin Rd. GL4
Colingbourne Rd. GL4
College Ct. GL1
College Fields. GL2
College Grn. GL1
College Rd. GL2
Coltman Clo. GL1
Columbia Clo. GL1
Colwell Av. GL3
Combrook Clo. GL4
Commercial Rd. GL1
Compton Clo. GL3
Concorde Way. GL4
Conduit St. GL1
Coney Hill Par. GL4
Coney Hill Rd. GL4
Coniston Rd. GL2
Constitution Walk. GL1
Conway Rd. GL3
Cooks Orchard. GL1
Coopers Elm. GL2
Coopers Vw. GL3
Copper Beech Gro. GL2
Copperfield Clo. GL4

32

ce Mews. GL4 20 D4
Clo. GL4 23 E3
ngley Clo. GL3 17 F5
der Dri. GL3 16 C3
roft La. GL4 24 C3
eld Dri. GL2 26 B3
ower Rd. GL4 20 B6
n Rd. GL2 22 D2
ation Grove. GL2 19 G2
old Gdns. GL4 16 A4
wold Rd. GL4 19 F6
Clo. GL4 25 F1
y Cres. GL1 19 F2
Gdns. GL2 18 A5
Pl. GL4 20 A5
Rd. GL3 26 B2
eld Rd. GL2 22 B5
Clo. GL3 20 D5
y Rd. GL4 23 G3
Way. GL4 20 C6
re Clo. GL3 20 D4
am Clo. GL4 25 E1
am La. GL3 17 F6
ell Clo. GL4 24 C2
Dri. GL3 16 D3
Rd. GL3 20 B3
ntdale. GL2 15 F3
Way. GL4 20 C2
raft La. GL3 17 F6
Clo. GL4 15 H4
Clo. GL3 17 F5
well St. GL1 18 D3
Keys La. GL1 13 C3
t. GL4 23 E2
y Rd. GL4 19 H6
Hayward Dri. GL2 22 B4

il Clo. GL4 20 B6
St. GL1 19 E4
lo. GL4 23 H1
an Clo. GL4 25 E1
y Rd. GL3 16 C3
Clo. GL2 15 H4
dale Clo. GL2 22 A5
Clo. GL2 22 B6
lo. GL2 22 B4
n Rd. GL4 24 A1
Way. GL2 26 C3
Row. GL1 14 D5
Ter. GL1 14 D6
Walk. GL1 14 D6
Way. GL1 14 D6
ark Rd. GL3 20 D3
urst Clo. GL4 25 E2
urst Pl. GL2 22 A5
ark Rd. GL1 15 E6
Ct. GL1 19 F3
Rd. GL1 19 F3
nt Clo. GL3 26 B2
d Clo. GL4 25 F1
s Clo. GL4 20 C5
s Clo. GL4 19 E6
ook Mews,
isdon Clo. GL4 25 E1
e Clo. GL2 26 B3
St. GL1 19 E3
well. GL3 20 C4
ery Rd. GL4 20 C6
gton Clo. GL4 20 A4
Walk. GL1 19 E5
y Rd. GL1 18 D5
Clo. GL1 19 E5
ale Clo. GL2 22 A5
dale Dri. GL2 16 A5
ng Way. GL3 17 F4
y Clo. GL2 22 A4
Clo. GL3 16 C2
n Way. GL4 24 C1
Clo. GL3 17 F5
Court. GL3 17 F5
noor. GL4 24 D2
Oak. GL2 22 B4
eadow La. GL3 15 H2
St. GL1 19 E4
f Beaufort Ct. GL1 23 F1
oft Rd. GL2 20 C2
Clo. GL2 22 A4
an Glen. GL3 17 F5
er Clo. GL4 23 E4
d Clo. GL3 15 H3
n Rd. GL4 19 H3
or St. GL1 19 E4

Way. GL4 19 H6
land Rd. GL4 23 G3
ott Way. GL3 16 D3

Eastbrook Rd. GL4 19 H4
Eastern Av. GL4 19 G5
Eastgate St. GL1 13 D3
Eastville Clo. GL4 19 G4
Ebor Rd. GL2 19 G2
Edgeworth Clo. GL4 25 E1
Edwy Par. GL1 14 D6
Elderberry Mws. GL3 16 C3
Eldersfield Clo. GL2 22 A4
Elderwood Way. GL4 23 E3
Eliot Clo. GL3 23 E2
Ellesmere Clo. GL3 20 C3
Ellison Clo. GL4 20 D6
Elm Dri. GL3 21 G5
Elmbridge Ct. GL3 16 B5
Elmbridge Rd. GL2 19 H2
Elmgrove Est. GL2 26 B3
Elmgrove Rd. GL3 20 C5
Elmgrove Rd East. GL2 26 A4
Elmgrove Rd West. GL2 22 A6
Elmira Rd. GL4 23 G1
Elmleaze. GL2 16 A6
Elmore La East. GL2 22 C3
Elmore La West. GL2 22 A3
Emerald Clo. GL4 23 E2
Empire Way. GL2 18 B6
Enborne Clo. GL4 23 F4
Ennerdale Av. GL2 15 H4
Epney Rd. GL3 23 E2
Ermin Pl. GL3 21 F5
Ermin St. GL3 21 F5
Erminster Dri. GL3 20 C4
Essex Clo. GL3 16 C1
Estcourt Clo. GL1 15 F5
Estcourt Rd. GL1 15 E5
Etheridge Pl. GL1 19 F2
Evenlode Rd. GL4 23 F4

Fairford Way. GL4 19 G5
Fairhaven Av. GL3 21 G5
Fairmile Gdns. GL2 15 E4
Fairwater Pk. GL4 20 A2
Fairways Dri. GL3 16 C1
Falcon Clo,
 Innsworth. GL2 15 H3
Falcon Clo,
 Quedgeley. GL2 22 C3
Faldo Clo. GL4 20 C6
Falfield Rd. GL4 23 F2
Falkner St. GL1 19 E3
Far Sandfield. GL3 17 F4
Faraday Clo. GL1 19 E5
Farm Mews. GL1 18 D4
Farm St. GL1 18 D4
Farmington Clo. GL4 25 E1
Farrant Av. GL3 16 D3
Farriers End. GL2 22 B4
Fennel Clo. GL4 24 D2
Fern Lawn. GL4 24 D3
Ferndale Clo. GL2 15 G4
Ferry Gdns. GL2 16 D2
Field End. GL3 20 C4
Fieldcote Dri. GL3 20 C4
Fieldcourt Dri. GL3 22 A5
Fieldcourt Farmhouse.
 GL2 22 B5
Fieldcourt Gdns. GL2 22 B6
Fielden. GL4 24 D3
Fieldfare. GL4 20 A6
Filbert Clo. GL4 24 D2
Filton Way. GL4 19 G5
Finch Rd. GL3 15 H3
Finchmoor Mews. GL2 15 E4
Finlay Pl. GL4 23 H1
Finlay Rd. GL4 23 G1
Fircroft Clo. GL3 20 C3
Fircroft Rd. GL2 15 E3
Firethorne Clo. GL4 15 G4
First Av. GL4 23 F3
Firwood Dri. GL4 23 G2
Flaxley Rd. GL4 23 F2
Fleming Clo. GL2 15 H3
Flower Way. GL4 15 G5
Foley Clo. GL4 23 F3
Folland Av. GL3 21 E5
Forbes Clo. GL4 20 C6
Forest View Rd. GL4 23 F3
Forsyte Way. GL4 19 G5
Forsythia Clo. GL3 16 C3
Fosse Clo. GL4 20 B5
Fourth Av. GL4 23 F3
Fox Clo. GL4 20 C6
Fox Run. GL2 22 C4
Fox Elms Rd. GL2 23 G3
Foxcote. GL2 15 G4
Foxglove Clo. GL4 20 B6

Foxleigh Cres. GL4 16 B4
Foxtail Clo. GL4 24 A1
Foxwell Dri. GL3 20 C4
Frampton Rd. GL1 18 C4
Fretherne Rd. GL3 23 F2
Friary Rd. GL4 20 B5
Frobisher Mews. GL3 16 C1
Frog Furlong La. GL2 16 B1
Fullers Ct. GL1 13 B2
Furlong Rd. GL1 18 D4
Furze Croft. GL2 22 B6
Gainsborough Dri. GL4 23 E4
Gambier Parry Gdns.
 GL2 15 E5
Gannet Clo. GL3 26 B2
Garden Way. GL2 15 G5
Gardiners Clo. GL3 16 D3
Garnalls Rd. GL4 24 C2
Gatmeres Rd. GL4 24 C3
Gatton Way. GL3 20 C2
Gazelle Clo. GL2 22 B3
George St. GL1 13 F3
George Whitfield Clo.
 GL4 24 C1
Georgian Clo. GL4 25 E2
Gere Clo. GL4 23 F4
Gibson Rd. GL3 16 B2
Gifford Clo. GL2 15 H4
Gilbert Rd. GL2 15 G4
Giles Cox. GL2 22 B5
Gilpin Av. GL3 20 C2
Gimson Clo. GL4 23 G1
Gladiator Clo. GL3 26 B2
Gladstone Rd. GL1 18 C5
Glencairn Av. GL4 23 E5
Glendower Clo. GL3 16 C1
Glenville Par. GL3 20 D4
Glevum Clo. GL2 15 G5
Glevum Way. GL4 24 D1
Gloucester M5 Southern
 Connector. GL2 22 C6
Gloucester Northern
 By-Pass, GL2 14 B5
Goddard Way. GL2 23 F4
Golden Clo. GL4 23 E3
Golden Vale. GL3 17 E3
Golden Valley
 By-Pass. GL3 16 B4
Goldsborough Clo. GL4 19 G5
Golf Club La. GL3 21 F5
Goodmore Cres. GL3 16 D3
Goodridge Av. GL2 22 C2
Goodyere St. GL1 19 E3
Gorse Clo. GL4 25 F1
Goss Wood Cnr. GL2 22 A5
Gothic Cott. GL1 19 E3
Gouda Way. GL1 13 C1
Grafton Rd. GL2 19 G1
Graham Gdns. GL1 15 F6
Grange Rd. GL4 23 E3
Granville St. GL1 18 C5
Grasby Clo. GL4 20 B4
Grasmere Rd. GL2 15 H5
Gray Clo. GL3 16 B2
Great Grove. GL4 20 A5
Great Western Rd. GL1 13 F2
Grebe Clo. GL4 24 D1
Green Acre. GL3 26 B2
Green Bank. GL3 26 B2
Green Clo. GL3 26 B2
Green Gdns. GL3 26 B2
Green La,
 Brockworth. GL3 26 D1
Green La,
 Churchdown. GL3 17 F5
Green La,
 Hardwicke. GL2 26 B3
Green La,
 Hucclecote. GL3 20 D5
Green Pippin Clo. GL2 19 H2
Green St. GL3 26 A2
Green Way. GL3 26 B2
Greenfields. GL3 16 C1
Greenhill Ct. GL4 22 D3
Greenhill Dri. GL4 22 D3
Greenville Clo. GL3 16 C1
Greenwood Clo. GL3 21 E5
Grenadier Clo. GL4 20 C5
*Greville Clo,
 Sandhurst Rd. GL2 14 D5
Greyfriars. GL1 13 C4
Greyhound Gdns. GL3 16 C3
Greyling Clo. GL4 25 E1
Grierson Clo. GL3 21 E5
Griffon Clo. GL3 22 C3
Grisedale Clo. GL2 15 H4
Grosvenor Rd. GL2 19 G1

Grove Cres. GL4 20 A2
Grove Rd. GL3 16 C4
Grove St. GL1 19 E4
Grovelands. GL4 20 B3
Guinea St. GL1 15 E6
Guise Av. GL3 26 C2
Guise Clo. GL2 22 B5
Gurney Av. GL4 23 F4
Hadow Way. GL2 22 B6
Hadrian Way. GL4 20 B5
Hailes Rd. GL4 20 A5
Hamer St. GL1 19 F2
Hammond Way. GL4 20 A2
Hampden Way. GL1 13 D4
Hampton Clo. GL3 21 E4
Hampton Pl. GL3 16 D1
Hanman Rd. GL1 19 F4
Hannah Pl. GL3 16 B2
Hanover Way. GL3 16 C2
Harbury Mews. GL1 19 F3
Hare La. GL1 13 D2
Harebell Pl. GL4 20 B6
Haresfield La. GL4 26 C4
Harewood Clo. GL4 23 E4
Harleys Field. GL4 20 A4
Harris Clo. GL3 17 E4
Hartington Rd. GL1 18 C5
Hartland Rd. GL1 19 E6
Harvest Way. GL2 22 B6
Harvey Clo. GL2 23 E1
Hasfield Clo. GL2 22 A4
Hatfield Rd. GL1 19 F4
Hathaway Clo. GL2 23 E2
Hatherley Rd. GL1 19 E5
Havelock Rd. GL3 20 D3
Haven Ct. GL2 19 H1
Hawk Clo. GL4 20 A6
Hawthorn Dri. GL3 16 C3
Hawthorne Av. GL4 19 H6
Haycroft Dri. GL4 24 D3
Haydale Gdns. GL2 15 H4
Hayes Ct. GL2 15 E3
Hayward Clo. GL4 20 A4
Hazel Clo. GL2 15 G4
Hazelcroft. GL3 16 D3
Hazelton Clo. GL4 19 E6
Headlam Clo. GL4 23 F4
Heath Dean Rd. GL3 16 C3
Heather Av. GL4 25 F1
Heathville Rd. GL1 15 E6
Hebden Clo. GL4 26 C2
Hembury Clo. GL2 22 A6
Hemmingsdale Rd. GL2 18 B3
Hempsted La. GL2 18 A5
Hendingham Clo. GL4 22 D3
Henley Pl. GL1 18 D6
Henry Rd. GL1 19 E1
Henry Ryder Clo. Gl4 20 C5
Henry St. GL1 19 E1
Herbert St. GL1 19 F3
Heron Way. GL4 19 H6
Hethersett Rd. GL1 19 F3
Hickley Gdns. GL3 26 B1
High Orchard St. GL1 18 C3
High St,
 Gloucester. GL1 19 E4
High St, Upton
 St Leonards. GL4 25 E4
High View. GL2 18 A5
Highbank Pk. GL2 15 E4
Highclere Rd. GL2 22 A4
Highfield Rd. GL4 19 G5
Highgrove Way. GL3 16 C2
Highliffe Dri. GL2 22 C5
Highworth Rd. GL1 19 E5
Hildyard Clo. GL2 26 C3
Hill Hay Rd. GL4 24 C3
Hill Rd. GL4 23 G2
Hillborough Rd. GL4 23 G3
Hillcot Clo. GL2 22 A4
Hillfield Court Rd. GL1 19 F1
Hillview Av. GL3 21 F5
Hillview Dri. GL3 20 C3
Hillview Rd. GL3 20 C3
Hilton Clo. GL2 18 A5
Hinton Rd. GL1 15 E5
Holham Av. GL3 17 E2
Holly End. GL2 22 C5
Holmleigh Rd. GL4 23 E3
Holmwood Clo. GL4 23 F4
Holmwood Dri. GL4 23 F4
Holst Way. GL4 23 F3
Homestead Ct. GL4 25 E1
Honeysuckle Dri. GL4 20 B6
Honeythorne Clo. GL2 18 A4
Honyatt Rd. GL1 19 E1

Hooper Clo. GL4 19 G5
Hopewell St. GL1 19 E3
Hornbeam Mews. GL2 15 G4
Horsebere Rd. GL3 20 D3
Horsley Clo. GL4 25 E1
Horton Rd. GL1 19 F2
*Howard Pl,
 Hucclecote Rd. GL3 20 D4
Howard St. GL1 18 D4
Howorth Clo. GL2 22 B3
Howcroft. GL3 17 F5
Howgate Clo. GL4 20 C6
Hucclecote Rd. GL3 20 B3
Humber Pl. GL3 26 C2
Hunters Gate. GL4 24 D2
Huntley Clo. GL4 20 B6
Hurcombe Way. GL3 26 B1
Hurst Clo. GL2 16 A4
Huxley Rd. GL1 19 E5
Hyde Clo. GL1 19 F1
Hyde La. GL1 19 E1

India Rd. GL1 19 F3
INDUSTRIAL & RETAIL:
Ashville Ind Est. GL2 18 B6
Gloucester
 Trading Est. GL3 21 E6
Innsworth
 Technology Pk. GL3 15 H3
Kings Walk Shopping.
 GL1 13 D3
Merchants Quay Shopping
 Centre. GL1 13 B4
Morelands
 Trading Est. GL1 18 C4
Olympus Park Business
 Centre. GL2 22 C3
St Oswalds
 Trading Est. GL1 14 D5
Waterwells Business Pk.
 GL2 26 D3
Innsworth La. GL2 15 H3
Insley Gdns. GL3 20 B3
Ivory Clo. GL4 23 E3
Ivy Mews. GL1 19 E6

Jackson Cres. GL3 16 C1
James Grieve Rd. GL4 20 C6
James Way. GL3 21 E5
Japonica Clo. GL3 16 C2
Jasmine Clo. GL4 23 F3
Javelin Way. GL3 26 B2
Jaythorpe. GL4 24 D2
Jenner Clo. GL3 20 C4
Jennings Walk. GL1 13 D4
Jersey Rd. GL1 19 E3
Jewson Clo. GL4 23 F4
John Daniels Way. GL3 17 E5
John Woods Alley. GL1 15 E6
Jordans Way. GL2 15 E4
Julian Clo. GL4 20 A3
Juniper Av. GL4 24 B2
Jupiter Way. GL4 20 C5

Katherine Clo. GL3 16 C1
Kaybourne Cres. GL3 17 G4
Keats Av. GL2 23 E2
Kemble Clo. GL4 23 F3
Kemble Rd. GL4 23 G2
Kencourt Clo. GL2 19 G1
Kendal Rd. GL2 15 H6
Kenilworth Av. GL2 19 F1
Kennedy Clo. GL3 20 C3
Kennet Gdns. GL4 25 E2
Kent Clo. GL3 17 G4
Kenton Dri. GL2 15 H4
Keriston Av. GL3 16 D3
Kestrel Gdns. GL2 22 B3
Keswick Clo. GL3 15 G6
Kevin Clo. GL4 20 A3
Kew Pl. GL2 15 H4
Kilminster Ct. GL3 16 D3
Kimberley Clo. GL3 16 A5
Kimbrose Way. GL1 13 C4
King Edwards Av. GL1 18 D5
Kingfisher Rise. GL2 22 A5
Kings Barton St. GL1 19 E2
Kings Sq. GL1 13 D3
Kings Walk. GL1 13 D3
Kingscote Clo. GL3 17 G5
Kingscote Dri. GL4 25 E1
Kingscroft Rd. GL3 20 C4
Kingsholm Ct. GL1 14 D5
Kingsholm Rd. GL1 13 E1
Kingsholm Sq. GL1 14 D6
Kingsley Rd. GL4 19 F6
Kingsmead. GL4 25 E1

Kingstone Av. GL3 20 B3
Kinmoor. GL4 24 D2
Kitchener Av. GL1 18 D6
Knollys End. GL2 22 B5
Knowles Rd. GL1 19 E4

Laburnum Gdns. GL2 22 B4
Laburnum Rd. GL1 23 F1
Lacca Clo. GL2 16 A4
Lacy Clo. GL2 15 H3
Lady Chapel Rd. GL4 20 B5
Ladybellegate St. GL1 13 B3
Ladysmith Rd. GL1 18 D6
Ladywell Clo. GL2 18 A5
Lambourn Clo. GL2 16 B6
Langdale Gdns. GL2 15 H4
Langley Rd. GL4 24 B1
Langton Clo. GL3 20 B3
Lanham Gdns. GL2 22 B6
Lannett Rd. GL1 18 D5
Lansdown Rd. GL1 15 E6
Larchwood Dri. GL4 23 G2
Larkham Clo. GL4 24 B3
Larkham Pl. GL4 24 C3
Larkhay Rd. GL3 20 D4
Larkspear Clo. GL1 18 D6
Lasne Cres. GL3 26 C2
Laura Clo. GL2 15 G5
Laurel Farm Clo. GL4 23 H1
Laurel Gate. GL4 25 F1
Lavender Vw. GL4 25 F1
Lavington Dri. GL2 16 B5
Lawrence Way. GL2 14 D6
Lawrence Way Nth. GL2 14 C5
Laxton Rd. GL4 20 D5
Laynes Rd. GL3 20 D4
Lea Cres. GL2 15 H4
Lea Rd. GL3 26 C2
Leacey Ct. GL3 16 D2
Leacey Mews. GL3 16 D2
Leadon Clo. GL3 26 C2
Leonard Rd. GL1 19 E5
Leven Clo. GL2 16 A5
Lewis Av. GL2 15 E3
Lewisham Rd. GL1 18 D6
Lichfield Rd. GL4 19 H3
Liddington Rd. GL2 16 B6
Lilac Way,
 Quedgeley. GL2 22 B4
Lilac Way,
 Tuffley. GL4 23 E3
Lilliesfield Av. GL3 20 B3
Lime Tree Ct. GL1 18 D6
Linden Rd. GL1 18 C5
Linnet Clo. GL4 24 C1
Linsley Way. GL4 23 F4
Lion Clo. GL2 22 B3
Little Awefield. GL4 24 C1
Little Elmbridge. GL2 16 A5
Little Normans. GL2 15 H4
Little Walk. GL2 15 H4
Littlefield. GL2 22 B4
Llandilo St. GL1 19 E4
Llanthony Rd. GL1 18 C2
Lobleys Dri. GL4 20 C6
London Rd. GL1 13 E2
Long Hope Clo. GL4 20 B6
Longborough Dri. GL4 25 E1
Longfield. GL2 22 B4
Longford La. GL2 15 E3
Longford Mews. GL2 15 E2
Longland Ct. GL2 15 G4
Longlands Gdns. GL2 15 G5
Longleat Av. GL4 23 E5
Longney Rd. GL2 23 F2
Longsmith St. GL1 13 C3
Longville Clo. GL4 25 F1
Lonsdale Rd. GL2 19 H1
Loriners Clo. GL2 22 B4
Lovage Clo. GL4 16 C3
Lower Meadow. GL2 22 B6
Lower Quay St. GL1 13 B2
Lower Tuffley La. GL2 22 D2
Luke La. GL3 16 B3
Lyng Clo. GL4 20 B3
Lynmouth Rd. GL3 20 C5
Lynton Rd. GL3 20 C5
Lysander Ct. GL3 17 F4
Lysons Av. GL1 18 C5

Madleaze Rd. GL1 18 C4
Magdala Rd. GL1 19 E3
Mainard Sq. GL2 15 G4
Maisemore Rd. GL2 14 A2
Maldon Gdns. GL1 19 E5
Malet Clo. GL2 15 H4

Mallard Clo. GL2 22 A4
Malmesbury Rd. GL4 19 F4
Malvern Rd. GL1 15 E5
Mandara Gro. GL4 24 D2
Mandeville Clo. GL2 15 H4
Manley Gdns. GL2 15 G4
Manor Gdns. GL4 20 B3
Manor Pk. GL2 16 B5
Mansell Clo. GL2 23 E1
Mansfield Mews. GL2 22 B6
Maple Ct. GL2 16 B5
Maple Clo. GL2 22 A6
Maple Dri. GL2 21 F4
Marefield Clo. GL4 20 B4
Marjoram Clo. GL4 20 C6
Marian Ct. GL1 13 B1
Market Par. GL1 13 E3
Market Way. GL1 13 D3
Marlborough Cres. GL4 19 F5
Marlborough Rd. GL4 19 F5
Marleyfield Clo. GL3 16 D2
Marleyfield Way. GL3 16 D2
Marram Clo. GL4 20 C6
Marten Clo. GL4 20 C6
Martindale Rd. GL3 16 D3
Marwell Clo. GL4 23 F5
Marylone. GL1 13 C3
Masefield Av. GL2 23 E1
Massey Pde. GL1 19 E5
Massey Rd. GL1 19 F5
Matson Av. GL4 24 C1
Matson La. GL4 24 B2
Matson Pl. GL1 19 F5
Maverdine Pass. GL1 13 C3
Mayall Ct. GL4 24 C3
Mayfair Clo. GL2 18 B4
Mayfield Dri. GL3 20 C3
Maytree Sq. GL4 19 H5
Mead Rd. GL4 20 B6
Meadow Way. GL3 17 E3
Meadowcroft. GL4 20 B6
Meadowleaze. GL2 16 A6
Meadvale Clo. GL2 15 E3
Medway Cres. GL3 26 C2
Meerbrook Way. GL2 26 C3
Meerstone Way. GL4 24 D2
Melbourne St East. GL1 19 E4
Melbourne St West. GL1 19 E4
Melick Clo. GL4 24 A1
Melody Way. GL2 16 B4
Melville Rd. GL3 17 E4
Mendip Clo. GL2 22 A5
Merchants Mead. GL2 22 A5
Merchants Rd. GL1 18 C3
Mercia Rd. GL1 14 D6
Mercury Way. GL4 20 C5
Merevale Rd. GL2 15 G6
Merlin Dri. GL2 22 B3
Meteor Way. GL3 26 B2
Metz Way. GL1 19 E2
Michaelmas Ct. GL1 15 F6
Middle Croft. GL4 20 A4
Middleton Lawn. GL3 16 B3
Midland Rd. GL1 18 D4
Milford Clo. GL2 15 G4
Mill Cnr. GL3 26 D2
Mill Gro. GL2 22 A5
Mill La. GL3 26 B1
Mill St. GL1 19 F3
Millbridge Rd. GL3 20 D4
Millbrook Clo. GL1 19 F3
Millbrook St. GL1 19 E3
Miller Clo. GL2 16 A4
Millers Dyke. GL2 22 A5
Millers Grn. GL1 13 C2
Millfields. GL3 20 D3
Millin Av. GL4 23 F3
Milo Pl. GL1 18 D5
Milton Av. GL2 23 E1
Minerva Clo. GL4 20 C5
Minster Gdns. GL4 20 B5
Minstrel Way. GL3 16 C1
Mogridge Clo. GL3 20 D4
Monarch Clo. GL4 25 E1
Monk Meadow. GL2 18 B4
Montford Rd. GL2 15 G4
Montgomery Clo. GL3 21 E5
Montpellier. GL1 18 D3
Montpellier Mews. GL1 18 D3
Moor St. GL1 19 E4
Moorfield Rd. GL4 26 B2
Moorhen Ct. GL2 22 A4
Morley Av. GL3 16 D3
Morpeth St. GL1 19 E4
Mortimer Rd. GL2 15 G4

Morton St. GL1 19 E4
Morton Cotts. GL1 19 E3
Morwent Clo. GL4 20 B6
Mosselle Dri. GL3 16 D3
Mottershead Dri. GL3 16 B2
Mount St. GL1 13 B1
Mowberry Clo. GL2 15 H4
Mulberry Clo. GL2 22 A6
Munsley Gro. GL4 24 C3
Mutsilver Mews. GL2 16 B4
Myers Rd. GL1 19 F2
Myrtle Clo. GL4 24 B1

Naas La. GL4 22 C6
Napier St. GL1 19 E2
Naunton Rd. GL4 20 A5
Nelson St. GL1 19 E5
Nene Clo. GL2 22 B3
Neptune Clo. GL4 20 C5
Netheridge Clo. GL2 22 C1
Nettleton Rd. GL1 13 E4
New Inn La. GL1 13 D3
New St. GL1 18 D4
Newark Rd. GL1 18 B5
Newland St. GL1 19 E1
Newstead Rd. GL4 20 B3
Newton Av. GL4 19 G5
Nicolson Clo. GL3 16 B2
Nine Elms Rd. GL2 16 B5
Noak Rd. GL3 21 G5
Noake Rd. GL3 20 D4
Norbury Av. GL4 24 B1
Norfolk St. GL1 18 C3
Norman Ball Way. GL1 19 F2
North Rd. GL1 15 E5
North Upton La. GL4 20 B4
Northbrook Rd. GL4 19 H2
Northfield Rd. GL4 19 E6
Northfield Sq. GL4 19 E6
Northgate St. GL1 13 D3
Notgrove Clo. GL4 23 E3
Notley Pl. GL4 20 D4
Nut Croft. GL4 19 G4
Nutley Av. GL4 23 E4
Nutmeg Clo. GL4 24 D2
Nympsfield Rd. GL4 23 F3

Oak Bank. GL4 23 G2
Oak Croft Clo. GL4 24 D3
Oak Dri. GL3 21 G5
Oak Tree Clo. GL2 26 B3
Oak Tree Gdn. GL4 24 C2
Oakhurst Clo. GL3 16 C4
Oakleaze. GL2 16 A6
Oakridge Clo. GL4 25 E1
Oakwood Dri. GL3 20 C5
Oatfield. GL2 22 B4
Old Cheltenham Rd. GL2 15 H5
Old Elmore La. GL2 22 D3
Old Painswick Rd. GL4 19 G5
Old Row. GL1 19 E3
Old Tram Rd. GL1 18 C3
Oldbury Orchard. GL3 17 F5
Olympus Park. GL2 22 C3
Orchard Clo,
 Hardwicke. GL2 26 B3
Orchard Clo,
 Walham. GL2 14 D4
Orchard Dri. GL3 17 F5
Orchard Park. GL4 20 D6
Orchard Rd. GL2 16 B5
Orchard Way. GL3 17 E2
Organs Alley. GL1 13 E4
Oriole Way. GL4 20 A5
Osborne Av. GL4 23 E4
Osbourne Clo. GL2 16 B6
Osier Clo. GL4 24 A1
Osprey Clo. GL4 20 A6
Osric Rd. GL1 19 E5
Otter Rd. GL4 24 A1
Over Causeway. GL2 14 A5
Overbridge Path. GL2 14 A6
Overbrook Clo. GL4 19 H3
Overbrook Rd. GL2 26 A3
Overbury Rd. GL1 19 F3
Owl Clo. GL4 20 A6
Oxford Rd. GL1 15 E6
Oxford St. GL1 13 F1
Oxford Ter. GL1 13 F2
Oxmoor. GL4 24 D2
Oxstalls Dri. GL2 15 F4
Oxstalls La. GL2 15 G6
Oxstalls Way. GL2 15 G5

Paddock Gdns. GL4 15 H4
Painswick Rd,
 Brockworth. GL4 26 C2

Painswick Rd,
 Saintbridge. GL4 19 G5
Palmer Av. GL4 25 F1
Park Av. GL2 15 H4
Park Dri. GL2 22 B5
Park Rd. GL1 18 D3
Park St. GL1 13 D2
Parkend Rd. GL1 18 D4
Parklands. GL3 22 B5
Parkside Clo. GL3 16 C3
Parkside Dri. GL3 16 C3
Parkwood Cres. GL3 20 C5
Parliament St. GL1 13 C4
Parr Clo. GL3 16 C2
Parry Rd. GL1 19 E5
Parton Dri. GL3 17 F4
Parton Rd. GL3 16 D2
Partridge Clo. GL2 23 E1
Patseamur Mews. GL2 16 B4
Paul St. GL1 19 E4
Paygrove La. GL2 16 A5
Paynes Pitch. GL3 17 F5
Peacock Clo. GL4 25 E1
Pear Tree Clo. GL2 26 B3
Pearce Way. GL2 22 D1
Peart Clo. GL1 19 F2
Pearwood Way. GL4 23 E3
Pegasus Gdns. GL2 22 B3
Pelham Cres. GL3 16 D3
Pembroke St. GL1 19 E3
Pembury Rd. GL4 23 G1
Pendock Clo. GL2 22 A4
Penhill Rd. GL4 24 B1
Pennine Clo. GL2 22 A6
Penny Clo. GL2 16 A5
Penrose Rd. GL3 16 A3
Percy St. GL1 19 E4
Peregrine Clo. GL2 22 B3
Perry Orchard. GL4 25 E4
Petworth Clo. GL4 23 E5
Philip St. GL1 18 C4
Piggy La. GL4 23 G4
Pilgrim Clo. GL4 20 B5
Pillcroft Clo. GL3 26 D2
Pillcroft Rd. GL3 26 D2
Pine Tree Drive. GL4 20 B4
Pinemount Rd. GL3 20 D4
Pinery Rd. GL4 20 B4
Pineway. GL4 19 G6
Pinewood Rd. GL2 22 A6
Pinlocks. GL4 25 E3
Pippin Clo. GL4 20 D6
Pirton Cres. GL3 17 E4
Pirton La. GL3 16 C3
Pirton Mdw. GL3 16 D4
Pitt Mill Gdns. GL3 20 D3
Pitt St. GL1 13 C1
Plock Ct. GL2 15 E4
Plum Tree Clo. GL4 25 E1
Podsmead Pl. GL1 18 C6
Podsmead Rd. GL1 23 F2
Poplar Clo. GL1 23 F1
Poplar Way. GL2 26 B3
Porchester Rd. GL3 20 C4
Portway. GL4 25 F5
Pound Clo. GL3 26 B2
Pound La. GL2 26 A4
Prescott Av. GL4 24 B1
Price St. GL1 18 C4
Primrose Clo. GL4 24 A1
Prince Albert Ct. GL3 21 F5
Prince St. GL1 13 F4
Prinknash Clo. GL4 24 C1
Prinknash Rd. GL4 24 C2
Priory Pl. GL1 13 C4
Priory Rd. GL1 13 C1
Purcell Rd. GL3 16 C1
Purslane Clo. GL4 24 B1

Quail Clo. GL4 20 B4
Quantock Rd. GL2 22 A6
Quay St. GL1 13 B2
Queens Clo. GL3 20 D3
Queens Walk. GL1 13 D4
Quenneys Clo. GL4 24 C3
Quinton Clo. GL3 17 E3

Raglan St. GL1 19 E3
Raikes Rd. GL1 18 C5
Raleigh Clo. GL3 16 C1
Ramsdale Rd. GL2 22 D2
Rance Pitch. GL3 25 E3
Randwick Rd. GL4 23 F3
Ranmoor. GL4 24 D3
Ravis Clo. GL4 19 G5
Rea La. GL2 18 A5
Rectory La. GL2 18 A5

Rectory Rd. GL4
Red Admiral Dri. GL4
Red Poll Way. GL4
Red Well Rd. GL4
Redding Clo. GL2
Redland Clo. GL2
Redstart Way. GL4
Redwing Way. GL2
Redwood Clo. GL1
Regent St. GL1
Remus Clo. GL4
Rendcomb Clo. GL4
Reservoir Rd. GL4
Ribble Clo. GL3
Richmond Av. GL4
Richmond Gdns. GL2
Ridgemount Clo. GL3
Rissington Rd. GL4
Rivermead. GL2
Rivermead Clo. GL2
Riversley Rd. GL2
Robert Raikes Av. GL4
Roberts Rd. GL3
Robinhood St. GL1
Robins End. GL3
Robinson Rd. GL1
Robinson Rd. GL2
Robinswood Gdns.
 GL4
Rockleigh Clo. GL4
Rodney Clo. GL2
Roman Rd. GL4
Romney Clo. GL1
Rookery Rd. GL3
Rosebery Av. GL1
Rosedale Clo. GL4
Rosemary Clo. GL4
Rowan Gdns. GL3
Royal Oak Rd. GL1
Rumsey Clo. GL4
Ruspidge Clo. GL4
Russell St. GL1
Russet Clo. GL4
Rustic Clo. GL4
Rydal Rd. GL2
Ryder Row. GL3
Ryecroft St. GL1
Ryelands. GL4

Sabre Clo. GL4
Saddlers Rd. GL2
Saffron Clo. GL4
Sage Clo. GL3
St Albans Rd. GL2
St Aldate St GL1
St Aldwyn Rd. GL1
St Ann Way. GL1
St Annes Clo. GL3
St Barnabas Clo. GL1
St Catherine Ct. GL1
St Catherine St. GL1
St Davids Clo. GL4
St Georges Clo. GL4
St Georges Rd. GL3
St James. GL2
St James Clo. GL2
St James St. GL1
St Johns Av. GL3
St Johns La. GL1
St Kilda Par. GL1
St Lawrence Rd. GL4
St Leonards Clo. GL4
St Lukes St. GL1
St Margarets Rd. GL3
St Mark St. GL1
St Marys Clo. GL4
St Marys Sq. GL1
St Marys St. GL1
St Michaels Sq. GL1
St Nicholas Sq. GL1
St Oswalds Rd. GL1
St Pauls Ct. GL1
St Pauls Rd. GL1
St Peters Rd. GL4
St Phillips Clo. GL3
St Swithuns Rd. GL2
St Vincents Way. GL3
Saintbridge Clo. GL4
Saintbridge Pl. GL4
Salisbury Rd. GL1
Salvia Clo. GL3
Sandalwood Dri. GL4
Sandfield Rd. GL3
Sandford Way. GL4
Sandhurst La. GL2
Sandhurst Rd. GL1
Sandown Lawn. GL3
Sandpiper Clo. GL2

34

gham Av. GL4	23 E4	Stanway Rd. GL4	19 H4
ir Clo. GL2	16 A4	Station App. GL1	13 F3
oft Rd. GL3	16 D2	Station Clo. GL3	17 F4
aze. GL2	19 H1	Station Rd,	
on Rd. GL4	19 E6	Churchdown. GL3	17 F5
e Clo. GL4	23 E1	Station Rd,	
Clo. GL4	20 C5	Gloucester. GL1	13 E3
ake Rd. GL4	19 F4	Staunton Clo. GL4	25 E1
Clo. GL2	15 H4	Steeple Clo. GL4	20 A4
le Mews. GL2	16 B4	Stevan Clo. GL2	17 F5
Cres. GL3	26 B2	Stewarts Mill La. GL4	25 E1
La. GL2	22 A6	Sticky La. GL2	26 B3
Mews. GL2	24 B1	Stirling Way. GL4	22 D3
. GL2	23 E1	Stockdale Clo. GL2	22 A5
ke Rd. GL1	15 E6	Stone Clo. GL4	20 B4
k Rd. GL3	26 B2	Stonechat Av. GL4	19 H6
St. GL1	15 E6	Stonehenge Rd. GL4	19 F4
Av. GL4	23 F3	Stow Clo. GL4	19 E6
Clo. GL4	23 E4	Stowell Mws. GL4	20 A4
Rd. GL4	23 H1	Stratford Clo. GL2	23 E1
d. GL1	14 D6	Stratton Rd. GL1	19 E3
cres. GL4	20 A5	Stroud Rd,	
Av. GL4	23 F3	Gloucester. GL1	18 C3
Oaks. GL2	22 B6	Stroud Rd,	
Rd. GL1	13 A4	Whaddon. GL4	23 G5
ale Dri. GL2	22 A5	Sudbrook Way. GL4	19 G6
ir Rd. GL1	18 C5	Sudgrove Clo. GL4	25 E1
ton Clo. GL3	17 E4	Sudgrove Park. GL4	25 E1
eare Av. GL2	23 E2	Sudmeadow Rd. GL2	18 A2
ck Clo. GL3	16 C3	Sulgrave Clo. GL4	23 E4
ater Gro. GL3	16 A3	Summerland Dri. GL3	17 F4
un Clo. GL2	16 A4	Sunderland Ct. GL4	24 D4
Av. GL2	23 E1	Sunnycroft Mews. GL1	23 G1
rd Rd. GL2	22 D2	Sunnyfield Rd. GL2	22 A6
rds Way. GL3	16 C2	Sussex Gdns. GL3	21 E4
rne St. GL1	15 E6	Swallow Cres. GL3	16 A3
Clo. GL4	24 D1	Swan Ct. GL1	13 B2
od Grn. GL2	15 E3	Swan Rd. GL1	15 E6
gton Rd. GL3	26 C2	Sweetbriar St. GL1	15 E6
St. GL1	19 F3	Swift Rd. GL4	20 A6
Clo. GL3	16 C2	Swordfish Clo. GL4	17 E4
irch Clo. GL2	22 B4	Sybil Rd. GL1	19 E5
lo. GL4	23 E3	Sycamore Clo. GL1	23 F1
ale Par. GL3	20 C3	Sydenham Ter. GL1	18 D5
ns Rd. GL3	20 C5		
Rd. GL2	15 G4	Tainmor Clo. GL2	16 B4
. GL2	22 C2	Talbot Mews. GL1	18 C6
St. GL1	19 E3	Tall Elms Clo. GL3	16 D4
End. GL2	19 H1	Tallis Rd. GL3	16 C1
Rd. GL2	19 H1	Tamar Rd. GL3	26 C2
lo. GL2	15 F3	Tandey Walk. GL3	16 B3
St. GL1	13 E1	Tanners Clo. GL3	26 B1
Way. GL4	19 G6	Tansy Clo. GL4	20 C6
St. GL1	19 E4	Tarlton Clo. GL4	25 E2
dge Rd. GL4	23 F3	Tarrington Rd. GL1	19 E5
ams Rd. GL4	24 B4	Taurus Clo. GL4	23 H2
on Gdns. GL3	16 D2	Taylors Ground. GL2	22 B4
op Clo. GL4	20 B6	Teal Clo. GL2	22 A5
ill Clo. GL4	20 B4	Teddington Gdns. GL4	19 G6
s Walk. GL3	21 E1	Telford Way. GL2	26 C3
et Pl. GL1	18 C3	Temple Clo. GL4	20 B3
Clo. GL4	24 A1	Tennyson Av. GL2	23 E1
lo. GL2	15 G5	Tern Clo. GL4	20 A5
ook Rd. GL4	19 H3	Tetbury Rd. GL4	23 G4
n Av. GL4	23 G2	Tewkesbury Rd. GL2	15 E4
ield Rd. GL4	23 G1	The Avenue. GL3	17 F4
ate St. GL1	13 B4	The Avenue. GL2	15 H5
GL1	18 C3	The Butts. GL4	24 A1
Clo. GL4	20 B5	The Causeway. GL2	22 A4
ell Clo. GL4	20 B6	The Chase. GL4	20 A6
r Clo. GL3	20 C4	The Chestnuts. GL1	18 C3
o. GL2	22 B3	The Conifers. GL1	19 F4
er Rd. GL2	18 B3	The Copse. GL4	20 B4
r Rd. GL4	20 B4	The Crescent. GL3	21 G5
ay. GL4	20 A3	The Dawes. GL2	22 C5
Eagle Rd. GL1	13 E2	The Dell. GL4	20 B4
ale Clo. GL2	22 A6	The Dukeries. GL1	13 B2
ield. GL2	22 B6	The Firs. GL1	15 E6
ell Gdns. GL3	17 E2	The Forum. GL1	13 D4
Clo. GL2	22 B6	The Furze. GL4	24 A1
Orchard. GL4	25 E2	The Hedgerow. GL3	15 G5
Meadow. GL2	15 E4	The Holly Grove. GL2	22 B6
y Mews. GL3	21 E5	The Holt. GL4	20 B4
a. GL2	26 A4	The Lampreys. GL4	19 G5
Rd. GL1	18 D5	The Laurels. GL1	19 E4
Ter. GL1	18 D5	The Lawns. GL4	24 D3
Walk. GL4	25 F4	The Lime. GL4	15 E4
or. GL4	24 D3	The Malverns. GL4	20 A6
r Cres. GL3	16 D3	The Manor. GL3	17 E5

The Maples. GL4	20 B5	Vulcan Way. GL4	20 C5
The Moat. GL2	22 B5		
The Noake. GL3	21 E3	Walham La. GL2	14 D5
The Oaks. GL4	20 B5	Walnut Clo. GL4	24 D2
The Orangery. GL4	20 B4	Walton Clo. GL4	25 E3
The Orchard. GL3	20 D5	Ward Av. GL3	16 B3
The Oval. GL1	18 C6	Warren Clo. GL3	16 D2
The Oxebode. GL1	13 D3	Warwick Av. GL4	23 E4
The Paddock. GL2	18 A5	Water Wheel Clo. GL2	22 A5
The Piece. GL3	17 F5	Waterdale Clo. GL2	22 A6
The Plocks. GL3	17 F4	Watermans Ct. GL2	22 A5
The Quay. GL1	13 A2	Watermeadow. GL2	22 B6
The Richmonds. GL4	24 D2	Watermoor Ct. GL3	16 D4
The Rudge. GL2	14 A1	Waters Reach. GL2	18 A5
The Stanley. GL4	25 F4	Waterside. GL2	22 A4
The Triangle. GL2	15 H6	Waterton Clo. GL3	21 E5
The Tulworths. GL2	15 G4	Waterwells Dri. GL2	26 D3
The Vines. GL3	20 D4	Watery La. GL2	25 F5
The Wayridge. GL4	24 D2	Watson Gro. GL4	25 F1
The Wheatridge. GL4	24 C1	Watts Clo. GL3	20 D5
The Willows. GL2	22 B4	Waverley Rd. GL2	19 G1
Theresa St. GL1	18 C4	Weald Clo. GL4	24 C1
Theyer Clo. GL3	26 B2	Weavers Rd. GL2	22 B4
Thomas Moore Clo. GL3	16 D1	Wedgwood Dri. GL2	15 H5
Thomas Stock Gdns. GL4	20 B5	Weir Bridge Clo. GL4	20 B3
Thomas St. GL1	19 E3	Well Cross Rd. GL4	24 A1
Thompson Way. GL3	16 A3	Welland Rd. GL2	22 B3
Thoresby Av. GL4	23 E5	Wellesley St. GL1	19 E5
Thornhill Clo. GL1	18 C6	Wellington Par. GL1	13 F2
Three Cocks La. GL1	13 C2	Wellington St. GL1	18 D3
Thrush Clo. GL4	20 A5	Wells Rd. GL4	19 H3
Thyme Clo. GL4	20 C6	Wellsprings Rd. GL2	15 G6
Tidswell Clo. GL2	22 B6	Welveland La. GL4	20 B3
Timmis Clo. GL4	24 C1	Wentworth Clo. GL2	15 G4
Tintern Rd. GL4	23 F2	West End La. GL3	21 E5
Tirley Clo. GL2	22 A5	West End Par. GL1	14 B6
Tone Dri. GL3	26 C2	West End Ter. GL1	14 B6
Towe Clo. GL4	20 A4	West Lodge Dri. GL4	20 A5
Trafalgar Dri. GL3	16 C1	Westbourne Dri. GL2	22 A6
Trajan Clo. GL4	20 C5	Westbury Rd. GL4	23 F2
Tredworth Rd. GL1	19 E4	Westcote Rd. GL4	23 G4
Trent Rd. GL3	26 C2	Westfield Av. GL3	21 F5
Trevor Rd. GL3	20 C5	Westfield Rd. GL3	21 F5
Tribune Pl. GL4	20 B5	Westfield Ter. GL2	14 D4
Trier Way. GL1	18 C3	Westgate St. GL1	13 A1
Trinity Rd. GL4	20 C5	Westland Rd. GL2	26 B3
Trubshaw Ct. GL3	17 E4	*Wesley Ct,	
Trygrove. GL4	20 A5	All Saints Rd. GL1	19 E3
Tudor St. GL1	18 C5	Westmead Rd. GL2	16 A4
Tuffley Av. GL1	18 B5	Weston Rd. GL1	18 D3
Tuffley Cres. GL1	18 B4	Westover Ct. GL3	16 D2
Tuffley La. GL4	22 D3	Whaddon Way. GL4	23 F5
Tweenbrook Av. GL1	18 D5	Wharfdale Way. GL2	22 A5
Twyver Bank. GL4	25 F3	Wheatridge Clo. GL4	24 D1
Twyver Clo. GL4	25 F3	Wheatstone Rd. GL1	19 E5
Tyndale Rd. GL3	25 F3	Wheatway. GL4	24 D2
Tynings Ct. GL3	17 F4	Whitebeam Clo. GL2	15 G4
		Whiteway Rd. GL4	24 B1
Ullenwood Rd. GL4	20 A4	Whitewell Clo. GL4	20 B3
Underhill Rd. GL4	24 C2	Whitfield St. GL1	13 E3
Union St. GL1	13 E1	Whittle Av. GL4	23 F4
Upper Quay St. GL1	13 B2	Whornes Orchard. GL4	25 E3
Upton Clo. GL4	20 B4	Widden St. GL1	19 E3
Upton Hill. GL4	25 F4	Wigmore Clo. GL4	20 B6
Upton La. GL4	25 E1	Wilkes Av. GL3	20 D3
Upton St. GL1	19 F4	Willow Av. GL4	19 G4
Usk Way. GL3	26 C2	Willow Croft Clo. GL4	24 D3
		Willow Way. GL4	19 G5
Valerian Clo. GL4	20 B5	Willowleaze. GL2	16 A6
Valley La. GL4	25 G5	Wilton Clo. GL2	18 C5
Vauxhall Rd. GL1	19 E3	Wilton Rd. GL1	18 C6
Vauxhall Ter. GL1	19 E3	Winchcombe Rd. GL4	23 G4
Vensfield Rd. GL2	22 B4	Winchester Dri. GL4	23 G3
Verbena Clo. GL4	20 B6	Windermere Rd. GL2	15 H5
Verburn Clo. GL4	25 F1	Windfall Way. GL2	19 H1
Vernal Clo. GL4	20 C6	Windmill Cotts. GL1	19 F3
Vertican Rd. GL3	16 A3	Windmill Field. GL4	20 A4
Vervain Clo. GL4	20 B6	Windrush Rd. GL4	23 G4
Vetch Clo. GL4	24 B1	Windsor Dri. GL4	23 E4
Viburnum View. GL4	25 F1	Winnycroft La. GL4	24 C5
Vicarage Clo. GL3	17 F5	Winsley Rd. GL4	24 C2
Vicarage La. GL3	20 D3	Winslow Pl. GL3	17 E3
Vicarage Rd. GL1	19 F4	Winston Rd. GL3	17 F4
Victoria Rd. GL2	15 E3	Wishford Clo. GL4	16 B5
Victoria St. GL1	19 E3	Wisteria Way. GL3	
Victory Clo. GL3	16 D3	Witcomb Clo. GL4	25 E3
Victory Rd. GL1	19 E5	Withy Mews. GL4	19 G6
Vincent Av. GL4	23 H2	Woburn Av. GL4	23 E4
Vine Ter. GL1	15 E6	Wolseley Rd. GL2	19 G1
Voyce Clo. GL4	23 F3	Woodbine Clo. GL4	20 B6

Woodcock Clo. GL4	20 A6
Woodcote. GL2	15 G4
Woodend Clo. GL4	20 B3
Woodford Clo. GL4	19 F5
Woodgate Clo. GL4	20 B4
Woodland Grn. GL4	25 E3
Woodpecker Rd. GL2	25 E1
Woodrow Way. GL2	22 D2
Woodruff Clo. GL4	24 B1
Woods Orchard. GL4	23 G4
Woods Orchard Rd.	
GL4	23 G4
Woolstrop Way. GL2	22 C2
Worcester Par. GL1	13 E1
Worcester St. GL1	13 E2
Wotton Ct. GL4	20 A2
Wotton Hill. GL2	19 F1
Wren Clo. GL4	19 G6
Wren Ter. GL3	16 A3
Wye Rd. GL3	26 C2
Yarrow Clo. GL4	24 A1
Yew Tree Way. GL3	16 D4
York Rd. GL4	19 H3
Zinnia Clo. GL3	16 C2
Zoons Rd. GL3	20 D3

SHURDINGTON

Atherton Clo. GL51	28 B2
Badgeworth La. GL51	28 A2
Bishop Rd. GL51	28 B1
Blenheim Orchard. GL51	28 C1
Church La. GL51	28 B1
Cowls Mead. GL51	28 B1
*Downfield Ho,	
Harrison Rd. GL51	28 B1
Farm La. GL51	28 B2
Greenway Clo. GL51	28 B2
Greenway La. GL51	28 B2
Gwinnett Ct. GL51	28 C1
Harrison Rd. GL51	28 B2
*John Lamb Ho,	
Atherton Clo. GL51	28 B2
Lambert Av. GL51	28 A2
Lambert Clo. GL51	28 B2
Lambert Dri. GL51	28 B2
Lambert Gdns. GL51	28 B2
Lambert Ter. GL51	28 B1
Laurence Clo. GL51	28 B1
Lawn Cres. GL51	28 C1
Leckhampton La. GL51	28 C1
Marsh Ter. GL51	28 B1
Robertson Rd. GL51	28 B1
School La. GL51	28 C1
Shurdington Rd. GL51	28 B2
Sinclair Rd. GL51	28 B2
The Orchard Gro. GL51	28 B2
Vicarage Clo. GL51	28 C1
*Welch Ho,	
Atherton Clo. GL51	28 B2
Wilson Rd. GL51	28 B2
Yarnolds. GL51	28 B2

www.ESTATE-PUBLICATIONS.co.uk
Red Books - showing the way

For the latest publication list, prices and to order online please visit our website.

LOCAL and SUPER RED BOOKS
(Super Red Books are shown in **Bold** Type)
Abingdon & Didcot
Aldershot & Camberley
Alfreton & Belper
Andover
Ashford & Tenterden
Aylesbury & Tring
Bangor & Caernarfon
Barnstaple & Bideford
Basildon & Billericay
Basingstoke & Andover
Bath & Bradford-upon-Avon
Bedford
Bodmin & Wadebridge
Bournemouth
Bracknell & Wokingham
Brentwood
Brighton
Bristol
Bromley (London Borough)
Burton-upon-Trent & Swadlincote
Bury St. Edmunds & Stowmarket
Cambridge
Cannock & Rugeley
Cardiff
Cardiff City & Bay Visitors Map (Sheet Map)
Carlisle & Penrith
Chelmsford
Chester
Chesterfield & Dronfield
Chichester & Bognor Regis
Chippenham & Calne
Coatbridge & Airdrie
Colchester & Clacton-on-Sea
Corby & Kettering
Coventry
Crawley & Mid Sussex
Crewe
Derby
Dundee & St. Andrews
Eastbourne
Edinburgh
Exeter & Exmouth
Falkirk & Grangemouth
Fareham & Gosport
Flintshire Towns
Folkestone & Dover
Glasgow
Gloucester & Cheltenham
Gravesend & Dartford
Grays & Thurrock
Great Yarmouth & Lowestoft
Grimsby & Cleethorpes
Guildford & Woking
Hamilton & Motherwell
Harlow & Bishops Stortford
Harrogate & Knaresborough
Hastings & Bexhill
Hereford
Hertford & Waltham Cross
High Wycombe
Huntingdon & St. Neots
Ipswich
Isle of Man
Isle of Wight (Complete Coverage)
Kendal & Windermere
Kidderminster
Kingston upon Hull
Lancaster & Morecambe
Leicester
Lincoln
Llandudno & Colwyn Bay
Loughborough & Coalville
Luton & Dunstable
Macclesfield & Wilmslow
Maidstone
Mansfield
Medway & Gillingham
Mid Wales Towns
Milton Keynes
New Forest Towns
Newbury & Thatcham
Newport & Chepstow
Newquay & Perranporth
Northampton
Northwich & Winsford
Norwich
Nottingham

Nuneaton & Bedworth
Oxford & Kidlington
Penzance & St. Ives
Perth
Peterborough
Plymouth
Portsmouth
Reading & Henley-on-Thames
Redditch & Bromsgrove
Reigate & Mole Valley
Rhyl & Prestatyn
Rugby
St. Albans, Welwyn & Hatfield
St. Austell & Lostwithiel
Salisbury & Wilton
Scarborough & Whitby
Scunthorpe
Sevenoaks
Shrewsbury
Sittingbourne & Faversham
Slough, Maidenhead & Windsor
Solihull
Southampton
Southend-on-Sea
Stafford
Stevenage & Letchworth
Stirling & Alloa
Stoke-on-Trent
Stroud & Nailsworth
Swansea
Swindon
Tamworth & Lichfield
Taunton & Bridgwater
Telford & Newport
Tenby & Saundersfoot (Colour)
Thanet & Canterbury
Torbay
Trowbridge & Frome
Truro & Falmouth
Tunbridge Wells & Tonbridge
Walsall
Warwick & Royal Leamington Spa
Watford & Hemel Hempstead
Wellingborough & Rushden
Wells & Glastonbury
West Midlands & Birmingham (Spiral)
Weston-super-Mare
Weymouth & Dorchester
Winchester
Wolverhampton (Sheet Map)
Worcester
Workington & Whitehaven
Worthing & Littlehampton
Wrexham
York

COUNTY RED BOOKS
(Town Centre Maps)
Bedfordshire
Berkshire
Buckinghamshire
Cambridgeshire
Cheshire
Cornwall
Cumbria
Derbyshire
Devon
Dorset
Essex
Gloucestershire
Hampshire
Herefordshire
Hertfordshire
Kent
Leicestershire & Rutland
Lincolnshire
Norfolk
Northamptonshire
Nottinghamshire
Oxfordshire
Shropshire
Somerset
Staffordshire
Suffolk
Surrey
Sussex (East)
Sussex (West)
Warwickshire
Wiltshire

Worcestershire

EUROPEAN STREET MAPS
Calais & Boulogne Shoppers Map (Sheet Map)
Dieppe Shoppers Map (Sheet Map)
North French Towns Street Atlas

OFFICIAL TOURIST MAPS and TOURIST MAPS
(Official Tourist Maps are shown in **Bold** Type)
- Kent to Cornwall 1:460,000
1 **South East England** 1:200,000
101 **Kent & East Sussex** 1:150,000
102 **Surrey & Sussex Downs** 1:150,000
103 South East England Leisure Map 1:200,000
104 **Sussex** 1:150,000
2 **Southern England** 1:200,000
201 Isle of Wight 1:50,000
3 **Wessex** 1:200,000
301 Dorset 1:150,000
4 **Devon & Cornwall** 1:200,000
401 **Cornwall** 1:180,000
402 **Devon** 1:200,000
403 **Dartmoor & South Devon Coast** 1:100,000
404 **Exmoor & North Devon** 1:100,000
5 Greater London (M25 Map) 1:80,000
6 **East Anglia** 1:200,000
7 **Chilterns & Thames Valley** 1:200,000
8 **Cotswolds & Severn Valley** 1:200,000
802 The Cotswolds 1:110,000
9 **Wales** 1:250,000
10 **The Shires of Middle England** 1:250,000
11 **The Mid Shires** (Staffs, Shrops, etc.) 1:200,000
111 **Peak District** 1:100,000
12 Snowdonia 1:125,000
13 **Yorkshire** 1:200,000
131 **Yorkshire Dales** 1:125,000
132 **North Yorkshire Moors** 1:125,000
14 **North West England** 1:200,000
141 **Isle of Man** 1:60,000
15 **North Pennines & Lakes** 1:200,000
151 Lake District 1:75,000
16 **Borders of Scotland & England** 1:200,000
17 **Burns Country** 1:200,000
18 Heart of Scotland 1:200,000
181 **Greater Glasgow** 1:150,000
182 **Edinburgh & The Lothians** 1:150,000
183 **Isle of Arran** 1:63,360
184 **Fife (Kingdom of)** 1:100,000
19 Loch Lomond 1:150,000
191 **Argyll, The Isles & Loch Lomond** 1:275,000
20 **Perthshire** 1:150,000
21 **Fort William, Ben Nevis, Glen Coe** 1:185,000
211 Iona and Mull 1:10,000 / 1:115,000
22 **Grampian Highlands** 1:185,000
23 **Loch Ness & Aviemore** 1:150,000
24 **Skye & Lochalsh** 1:130,000
25 **Argyll & The Isles** 1:200,000
26 **Caithness & Sutherland** 1:185,000
27 **Western Isles** 1:125,000
28 **Orkney & Shetland** 1:128,000 } same map
28 **Shetland & Orkney** 1:128,000 }
30 **Highlands of Scotland** 1:275,000
92 England & Wales 1:650,000
93 Scotland 1:500,000
94 Historic Scotland 1:500,000
95 Scotland (Homelands of the Clans)
99 Great Britain 1:1,100,000
99 Great Britain (Flat) 1:1,100,000
100 British Isles 1:1,100,000

EUROPEAN LEISURE MAPS
Europe 1:3,100,000
Cross Channel Visitors' Map 1:530,000
France 1:1,000,000
Germany 1:1,000,000
Ireland 1:625,000
Italy 1:1,000,000
Netherlands, Belgium & Luxembourg 1:600,000
Spain & Portugal 1:1,000,000

WORLD MAPS
World Map - Political (Folded) 1:29,000,000
World Map - Political (Flat in Tube) 1:29,000,000
World Travel Adventure Map (Folded) 1:29,000,000
World Travel Adventure Map (Flat in Tube) 1:29,000,000

ESTATE PUBLICATIONS, Bridewell House, Tenterden, Kent. **TN30 6EP**
Tel: 01580 764225   Fax: 01580 763720   Email: sales@estate-publications.co.uk

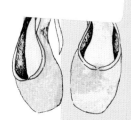

Rhythmic Rhymes
for Dancers

Written by **Carolyn Rathgeb**

Copyright © **Carolyn Rathgeb 2008**

All right reserved. No part of this publication
may be reproduced, stored in a retrieval
system, or transmitted in any form or by any
means – electonic, mechanical, photocopying,
recording or otherwise – without prior
permission from the author.

Published by **Carolyn Rathgeb**
Brixham, Devon

Illustrations by **Georgina Stroud**

Designed and Printed by
BPR The Printers, Paignton, Devon

ISBN No. 978-0-9561170-0-7

Acknowledgements

Thanks to my husband Rolf
and daughter Avalon.

Thanks for letting me use your names
within my poems to:

Bird College, London;

Gillian Hurst, Royal Ballet School;

Anne Clark, Secretary of the British Ballet
Organisation;

Deborah Clark, Senior Examiner and Head
of Tap for the British Ballet Organisation.

Introduction

Having trained from being small as a dancer,
I travelled all over the world dancing in
many different countries and working on
many different cruise ships.
I ran my own dance school for eighteen
years and am currently a Senior Examiner
for the British Ballet Organization.

I have written these amusing rhymes as
reflections on my vast experiences.
The range of my book is aimed at from
eight to Adult.
It is my hope that these rhymes bring as
much enjoyment and encouragement to
each reader and dancer as I have
experienced in writing them.

Happy dancing, Carolyn.

In a Spin

"Pirouettes today"
"Hooray hooray….."
My favourite thing" shouts Katy Gray.
"Calm down pupils, let's form lines
Ahead will be some trying times"

"Altogether, find a spot
In front of you, maybe a dot.
Turn your body, leave your head
Now whip and find your spot, that said….."

Arms to third, seconde and first
Keep them level like Gillian Hurst
Joe, your turns they are improving.
Come on people, keep things moving.

Don't forget to retire'
Bettering technique every day
I'd prefer a single not a double
That's why Amelia you're in trouble.

Getting better, one two three
Oops Avalon's fallen, hurt her knee
She's getting up without a word
Now performing triples at Doreen Bird".

Baby Class Interrupted

Well hello my darlings
Now let us begin
Our ballet this evening
With a great big grin.

Hello to Annabel, Sophie and Kim
Hello to Richard, Polly and Jim.
That's O.K. Grandad, I'll do Rachel's hair
Yes her ribbons as well, now she's in my care.

Let's make a big circle
And stand oh so tall
Feet parallel;
Jade, not facing the wall!

Christopher Hargreaves
I've told you before
Please don't kiss Jenny
Until half past four.

Well that's a small circle
Let's take two steps back
Knees are pulled up,
Don't do that Jack!

Plie' and stretch
Rise on our toes
Thank you Mrs Harper
4/4 is what goes.

Pulling up tummies
Rounding our arms
Bras bas to first, now right up to fifth
Let's balance, all balance, holding that pose.

Time now my darlings
To sit on the floor
To practise our frogs
And our beetles galore.

Christopher Hargreaves
Once more and I will
Stand you in the corner
And make you stand still.

Did you all hear the story
Of a Prince and Princess?
They met at the Ballet
It was quite a success.

So, girls over here
And boys to the front
Let's pretend to be them
Oh Sophie, don't grunt.

Are we looking gorgeous?
All stretching our feet
Boys bow, girls curtsey
Are we on the beat?

Hello Mrs Hargreaves
Yes, we are almost done
Kiss Jenny?...Of course not
He's a wonderful son!

Opening Routine

Five, six, seven, eight
Shuffle hop step
Smile! Be great!

Tapstep ballchange
Shuffle toe heel
Keep tapping on
It's no big deal.

The lights are on
Pick hop, Pick hop
Tapstep ballchange
Shuffle stamp drop.

Jazz hands, jazz hands
Hop flap ballchange
Tapstep, step kick
Finish.....step click.

A Performer's Vocation

Vocational School is simply fab
Hard work though, but never drab
Teachers strive to better us
Students dance without fuss.

In the process of our goal
Precisely mastering each role
One day we act, sing and shout
Ballet the next, with full turn-out.

Requirements differ every day
To demonstrate alacrity
Altogether aiming for
Perfect performers ever more.

I'm only six and......

It's opening night
I'm getting stage fright
I must calmly remember
Not to be uptight.

I have to stretch my knees
And point my toes
Smile at my Mum and Dad
And Gran as it goes.

My music has started
My legs won't move
I've forgotten my steps
But I must improve.

A big breath in
Then out again
Hop chasse' and bouree'
In line with Elaine.

I'm feeling calm
Without alarm
Lifting arms to fifth
With graceful charm.

Changement, soubresaut
Changement and hold
Step and curtsey
I was oh so bold!

Improvise Guys

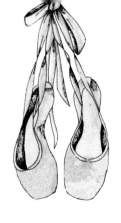

Tapspring kick hop
Shuffle step ballchange
In our tap class
We do the whole range.

Triple Wings and Riffs
That go up to thirty
Toe heel step spring dig.....
Get it right Gertie.

Kick heel step heel
Step heel kick
Shuffle ballchange drop
Step spring flick.

Double Pick up
Zip tap drop
Tickle the floor
Loosen knees, tap hop.

We can't give up now
Or lose the plot
Mr Sroka's coming in
But our dance is hot
Well we think it is
But, he might not.

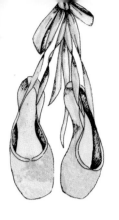

Heartfelt Art

Body Conditioning is serious indeed
It relies upon the teacher
For each individual need.

For strengthening and stretching
To be lithe beyond compare
Daily exercise
Is every dancer's fayre.

Warming up thoroughly's
Essential and a must
It will earn us later
A hopeful happy crust.

To be fit and agile
Is insurance for our art
But to be a good dancer
Comes from deep within the heart.

Distinction for Head Quarters

In the office of H.Q.
Coordinating points of view
Which dates for Dance Days should we choose?
Which leotard colour, greens or blues?

When should we plan Ballet Majors?
Council meetings taking ages
Paper work to keep us going
Computers now keep it flowing.

It's all a matter of combining
Membership thoughts not undermining
Everybody's point of view
With Anne Clark's help to see us through.

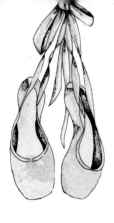

Life on Stage

Life's eccentricities
Revealed upon the Stage
The audience is entertained
By sweeping swirling lines.

Circles within circles
And spirals with inclines
Constant flowing movements
Performed to beating chimes.

Several ladies dressed in black
Two men wearing white
Floating fabrics, casting shadows
Curtains masking light.

Walking, running, spinning turns
A counterbalanced pose
Squares and oblongs, triangles
A concentric circled rose.

Commencing slowly, building speed
Stories being told
Of distant lands with tragic tales
Ever unfolding lore.

Conclusions slowing pace
Spacing shapes upon the ground
Silence, then with calm and still
The end, now being found.

My Friend Kate

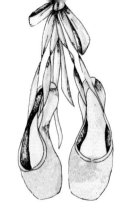

I'm jealous of my friend
She's better at tap
I always try so hard
But never sound like that.

She always comes in late
Never on time
But I'm in early
And on the front line.

Miss Anne gets upset
When my beats are flat
Though I'm thinking of tea
I can't deny that.

Chicken pie with peas
Mango fruit crumble
Now that's in my head
My tummy's a rumble.

"Wake up Honey
You've missed your turn
I don't think that
You'll ever learn

To stay with the timing
And concentrate
Or to be very good
Like your friend Kate!"

Stepping Down and Out

It's off to Jazz Class now I go
Jazz shoes and catsuit all in tow
As I push on the studio door
It opens up, revealing more.....

Plie' than I have seen all day
In tap or modern, but that's okay
As the real Jazz style is very down
For the centre lowered, it is renowned.

Replace the left foot with the right,
Stay long and low and pulled up tight,
Dance to the drums and feel the beat
Enjoy the rhythms with your feet.

A Dancer's Pointe of View

Rising up through backs of toes
No pain at all as it goes
Starting slowly getting quicker
In the eyes, not a flicker

Of a thought within a head
To fill a dancer with great dread
That is, of course as you well know
Exclusion from the looming show

Bouree's and pose's are now needed
Miss Pam's words must well be heeded:
"I don't want to see at all
Baggy knees within this hall
Please pull up tums, make movements light
I'd like you soon to get it right.

Imagine then being Centre Stage
Where Corps de Ballet's all the rage
Think Covent Garden, dressed in white
With that thought you'll be alright.

Through the curtains on you go
Smiling nicely to each row
Keep it going, looking good
I really knew, you always would!".

Continuing Enchainement

Tendu plee e ay
Tendu and a bend
Tendu plee e ay
Stretch toes right to the end.

Point devant, fifth, seconde
Fifth derriere, fifth and hold
Point derriere, fifth, seconde
Fifth devant, now let's be bold.

Let's take a dev el o pay devant
Then chasse' en avant
Pose' derriere to fifth en pointe
Raise arms to fifth as well.

Bouree' on the spot
Retire' and lower
Bouree' on the spot and hold.

Demi detourne'
Ports de Bras
Now repeat what you've been told.

Tendu........

To Beat or not to Beat

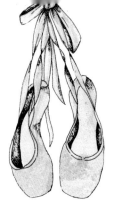

Let's get our batterie sorted out
Improve we must, or there's no doubt
At next exam with Miss D. Clark
She'll get upset and then will mark
Our reports with her flat remark:
'Keep practising with which you'll see
An improvement, which great will be'.

So week by week onward we strive
And beat we must or not survive
Our teacher's wrath in overdrive
Fuelled on for sure in knowing that
Each beat must have correct format.

Changement battu, entrechat
To practise these, it's to the barre
Plie' then spring into the air
Feet seconde, now beat en l'air

When alighting remember
So no injuries occur
Knees must be over toes
Now we're perfect
Exam.....here goes!

A Magical Evening

A night at the Ballet
With Sally and Garrie
Excitement backstage
With a front of house hum.

The lights are now lowering
The orchestra powering
Instruments squeakily
Tuning them in.

The curtains whoosh open
Revealing a scene
With a river and woodland
All painted in green.

Dancers glide by in muslin and tulle
A Prince and his maiden, joyful until
An evil one enters
Bringing gloom to the fore.

Much rowdiness follows
With fighting and scuffles
The crowd scene is vibrant
Concluding a sword dance, artistically won

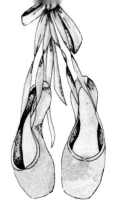

By friends of the Prince
Now swaggering, drunken,
The evil one thwarted
Not having much fun.

The King and his Queen
Send out invitations
Villagers revelling
Happy, elated
Celebrating the wedding
Of the Prince and his 'one'.

The stage is now silent
The music has ceased
The house lights glimmer
The audience pleased.

To have shared an adventure
In a far off place
Now only memories remain
Of culture and grace.

The Dancer

Life is dance
And dance is life
The essence of
Each day to day.

Agonies of realities
Are pushed aside
By releasing the dreams
That lay inside
The Dancer.

Underneath the Dancer's Shoe

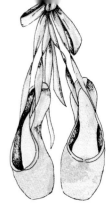

Tap plates, ballet soles
Let's marry them together
Linking by design and fate
A pulsing heart forever.

Intricate sparkly shoes of leather
Holding secrets of the wearer
Detailed, curving lines all joined
Wishing luck upon the bearer

Backstage Collywobbles

Patiently waiting backstage nervously
Contemplating sequences of footsteps earnestly.
Should it be a single or a double or a kick?
No – I've got it sorted out; a cartwheel into split.

Now I've thought the footwork through,
where should I go?
Was it downstage right or left,
Or was it to and fro?

If I just let my mind go blank
And concentrate on air,
An angel flutters through my thoughts
And dances everywhere.

So now remembering everything,
My inner self is calm
The audience is waiting
With applause that's oh so warm.

Gliding trancelike
Drifting through my dreams
A fairy lands upon my toe
And I wake up with a scream.

Into reality – awake within a flash
"you're late" shouts Mum
She's looking glum
And down the road I dash

....to class!

Teenager's Delight

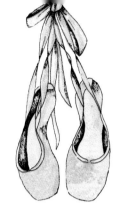

My teenage tap class began pleasantly
Dan and Holly commenced willingly
You see last week they sat outside
And argued by the door
About who would be first to start
Amalgamation Four.

Tackling Timesteps, the door is opened wide
"Look Miss, at Poppy's hair
Cut short, spikey and dyed.
Bright blue with green and yellow streaks
She wanted that for weeks
It's cool Miss, but not Miss
As cool as your pink quiff!"

The Rhythm of Dance

The rhythm of dance
Is life indeed
And dancers dance
To fill a need.

To express inside
The feeling of
Complete abandon
Of worldly worries
Best forgotten.

Little Dancer

Little dancer
Big show
Mum and Dad
Front row.

The Rumbles

When is it tea time?
When will this lesson end?
The teacher today is
Driving me round the bend.

How many times have I
Practised pas de chat?
They must be getting better now
I really think they are.

Up up down, up up down
Keep that footwork neat
"Please remember arms girls
And do stay with the beat".

I love it really, so I do
But the thought within my head
Is what my Mum has baked for tea
I hope it's home made bread

The Inevitable

When examining last year
It soon became clear
That candidate two
Really needed the loo.

On enquiring if she
Wanted to go quickly
Crossed legs were a struggle
On the floor, a puddle.

The Dancer's Wish List

A dancer's wish is to perform
Movement
Enhanced by music
Sympathetically lit.

To express to an audience
In front of a stage
Blending sounds
And coordinated motions

To perform each piece
With qualities unequalled
Unrivalled by another
Are the requirements one craves.

Sad Pointes

My old pointe shoes hanging from a hook
Helped me gain Distinction in the last exam I took.

They were really strong and supple
as I put them through their paces
Supported me for releve's
With tightly sewn on laces.

My darning was a giveaway
I'm not so good at stitches
But they stopped me skidding round the room
Not showing any glitches.

My old pointe shoes now full of dust
In their corner hanging sadly
Feeling deep disgust
At their owner's oblivion
Of their existence
Without her they won't 'ere again
Feel the thrill of dance

Night after Night

I absolutely love it here
Dancing is my right
In the studio practising
Night after night.

My friends say I'm sad
I think they're mad
Not to dance or even
Go to 'Street with Stephen'.

I was lucky with my latest heat
Of auditions in Spring
The producer said he found quite neat
My enthusiastic grin.

And so I hope to see you all
On the West End in the Fall
Rehearsals first of course and then
Comps in rows of ten!

An artistic flair

Contemporary Dance
Is an art form
All it's own.

Visionary depictions
Of a storyline unfold.

Each step reveals
A jigsaw part
Of one much bigger plan.

To build up a creative piece
Expanding lines upon
Movements and emotions
A narrative within.

Leaping bounding energies
That spiral and then spin
Twisting, curling, lifting shapes
Patterns flowing on.

Concluding when the tale is done
And motions are all gone.

Imminent Classes

I begged my Mum
When I was young
To take me to Dance Class
She told me that I had to wait
Until my Dad came in.

I tidied up.
I washed the pots.
I even bathed the dog
I took my brother Peter out
And was nice to his pet frog.

In Dad came
Drenched in rain
Not in the best of mood
And announced that I could dance next week
If he was given food!

Ships at Sea

We had fun
Dancing upon
Ships at sea
My friends and me.

Happy years
Without fears
Seeing places
And different races.

We cruised around
A world unfound
Locations
Undiscovered.

But best of all
As we set sail
The Can Can
Revered without fail.

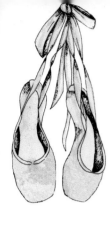

Summer Heat

At the festival in June
To a rather dubious tune
I sat and watched aghast
Proceedings yet unmasked.

A tiny duet
Not quite finished yet
Rudely interrupted
By a rival team.

Entering loudly
Not talking cowardly
In the auditorium
Causing mayhem.

Silently adjudicating
Audience waiting
For the results
Of the latest heat.

Now lined up
Standing with a card
All the contestants
That have tried so hard.

In their quest
To be best
The rival side
Are disqualified.

The results are in
The couple to win
Excelling with flair
Are our tiny pair!

Ballet Heaven

When I drift off to sleep at night
My mind wanders to a place all white
With floating clouds and fairies light
Of step with stature very slight.

Angels fly in floating chiffon
Satin shoes with silken ribbon
Footwork emitting natural rhythm
Dances show perfect precision.

In my dreams of self perception
Of no mistakes in recollection
A willowy spirit is my reflection
Ballet heaven: the ideal location.

Silvery Skies

From the tap plate up
To the ballet sole on high
With the pulse of the beat
Residing in the silver sky.

Of the semi circulation
In our dance wide nation
Linking ballet dance and tap
In our worldly dance elation.

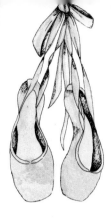

The Finale`

The best is saved until the last
Fleeting glimmers of a show all passed
An upbeat dance including all
The collective cast standing tall.

Waiting in anticipation
A united bow in trepidation
Hoping now that front of house will
Give applause to thrill.